Secret
Donuts

Secret Donuts

A JOURNEY TO GETTING OVER YOUR WEIGHT, ALIGNED WITH GOD AND INTO YOUR PURPOSE

ALICIA L. WATSON

SECRET DONUTS
Published by Purposely Created Publishing Group™
Copyright © 2019 Alicia Watson
All rights reserved.

No part of this book may be reproduced, distributed or transmitted in any form by any means, graphic, electronic, or mechanical, including photocopy, recording, taping, or by any information storage or retrieval system, without permission in writing from the publisher, except in the case of reprints in the context of reviews, quotes, or references.

Scriptures marked NIV are taken from the New International Version®. Copyright © 1973, 1978, 1984, 2011 by Biblica, Inc.™. All rights reserved.

Scriptures marked NLT are taken from the New Living Translation®. Copyright © 1996, 2004, 2007, 2013 by Tyndale House Foundation. All rights reserved.

Scriptures marked TNIV are taken from The Holy Bible, New International Version. Grand Rapids: Zondervan House, 1984. Print.

Printed in the United States of America

ISBN: 978-1-949134-59-9

Special discounts are available on bulk quantity purchases by book clubs, associations and special interest groups. For details email: sales@publishyourgift.com or call (888) 949-6228.

For information log on to www.PublishYourGift.com

Table of Contents

Foreword vii
Prologue: Why "Secret Donuts" xi

Part I: Maybe You're Like Me (My Story) 1
   1. How Did I Get Here? 3
   2. How Do I Get Out of Here? 19
   3. Can't Serve Both God and... 23
   4. We Need to Make a U-Turn 33
      a. For Richer or Poorer; Through Backrolls
         and Snatched-Waistedness 33
      b. Love Is the Greatest 40
      c. Yo! Who Raised Y'all? Oh Wait, I Did 42
      d. Hustle & Grinding My Gears 50

Part II: Okay, It's Time to Check the Map 59
   5. Getting over Our Weight and into Our
      Purpose 61
   6. So, What's Your Purpose? 67
   7. No, Seriously, He's Sending You—Yes, You! .. 75
   8. If God Is for You 89
   9. For Such a Time as This 99
  10. Obedience Is Better, Trust Me 109

Part III: From God's Love to Self-Love 119
  11. Do You See These Gains? 119
  12. Feel Great, Look Great 125
  13. These Snacks Ain't Loyal 139
  14. What's It Going to Be? 149

Afterword: My Before and After 159
About the Author 163

Foreword

Food is a four-letter word that wields great influence. Our lives are either enhanced or diminished by food depending on its level of importance. So, if you are you are preoccupied with food, please continue reading.

A wise man once said, "One should eat to live, not live to eat." When a person eats to live, the focus is eating for nourishment, allowing food to have its proper place and not be a main source of pleasure. Otherwise a person can possibly experience overconsumption.

We all know that too much of anything can be detrimental; living a balanced life is what matters. For example, our bodies use balance to evenly distribute weight to help us to remain upright and steady. When balancing food, let's consider the words of Jesus: "Man shall not live on bread alone, but on every word that comes from the mouth of God" (Matthew 4:4 NLT). While physical food is essential for maintaining life, spiritual food (the Word of God) is essential for meeting our goals, fulfilling our purpose, and overcoming obstacles in life.

External solutions don't always solve internal problems. You might hear a voice inside your head promising a better life when you lose the extra 30 pounds, fit into that little black dress, or have abs as hard as steel. This is a deceptive mindset that makes us feel better about our internal self.

The Bible warns that deceptive thinking can lead to idolatry and sinful behavior. For example, Eve was deceived, and sin was the result. Simply put, she heard that voice inside her head promising a better life filled with secret knowledge, divine wisdom, and immortality. She believed the lie that said, "It's all about me, and it's for my glory; I shall be like God." While this example may seem extreme, it's not a stretch of the imagination.

In a culture that celebrates the slender-frame body, it's easy to internalize the message that when you're slender or skinny, you're more valuable as a person.

In *Secret Donuts*, Alicia debunks the deceptive internal messages that keep women distracted, deceived, obscure, and bound to idols unaware. Alicia not only shares her personal obsessive encounters with food, but also the impact of weight on one's self-esteem. I encourage you, the reader, to walk with Alicia on her journey of secrets, fear, the moment of truth, vulnerability, lessons learned, and life today. This is not another self-help book on how to change you for the better. It's more like a conversation over coffee with a good honest friend that could change your life!

Reading the book will take you on a very personal yet familiar journey of preoccupation with food and self-esteem issues. Alicia's story has revealing beginning and ending points that reflect the struggles with self, others, and God. She has a unique and inclusive voice that communicates to the reader, "You are not alone, and we're in this together." As a pastoral counselor working with people struggling with eating disorders, body image issues, and weight management, I implore you to pay attention to what Alicia has learned. Her truth is centered on God's truth and will help to set you free!

In a 2016 study, the *International Journal of Behavioral Medicine* examined the developmental course of self-esteem and body mass index (BMI) on women from adolescence to mid-adulthood. The study traced the association between self-esteem and BMI over a 26-year period. The authors discovered that the higher their body mass index, the poorer the participants felt about themselves. The study proves that self-perception or the way we see ourselves has great impact on our self-esteem. For this reason, interventions are needed to tackle weight-related stigma, and reading this book is a great start. Be blessed as you read.

Rev. Trina Goffe
Pastoral Counselor, Author, Speaker

PROLOGUE

Why "Secret Donuts"?

"Hey, I'll be back. I'm going to the store to get some {thinks quickly}, uh, laundry detergent."

I say this to my husband as I grab my keys and head out of the door, into my car, and down the street on my way to the grocery store.

When I get there, I make a beeline for the bakery section, grab not one but two donuts, and toss them in the clear plastic bag, intentionally ignoring their posted calorie counts. My mouth begins to water.

I go to aisle four, grab some laundry detergent, throw it in the cart, and check out. Back in the car, I slide my hand into the bag for the first squishy, chocolatey delight as I pull out of the parking lot, music blasting and shoulders shimmying. Who else dances when they get good food? Just me? Okay.

Before I get to the first light (and before I even know it), the second donut is in my hand heading towards my mouth, and I bite into its lemon-filled glory. I hit the third light and make a right turn toward my neighborhood. I drive right on past my street. I arrive at the convenience store a few blocks away, swing open my door, and toss all evidence in the trash can outside their door. Then I go home.

See? Secret donuts. Literally.

I titled this book *Secret Donuts* because anyone who struggles with their weight and reads this book will immediately understand what I meant without explanation. If this is not your struggle, then the story I shared might sound really funny or even absurd to you, but I want to set the tone for this book. This won't be a self-help book with pages of me talking at you and telling you what to do; this will be more like a conversation and an exercise in humility, transparency, and vulnerability. Think of it as something akin to a memoir. I'm sharing my experiences and lessons with the hope that this book will set me free (as I write it) and the readers free (as you read it).

Free from what, you ask? Well, free from shame; from fear; from any obstacle that stands in the way of you pursuing your purpose, of you knowing that you are enough just as you are; and from putting too much weight on your weight. I want to be and I want you to be free from hiding what you do and from hiding who you are.

It's a real struggle sometimes as I go along this journey of writing this book. My instruction from God going into 2018 was that I was not allowed to focus on losing weight. Listen, I legit heard that I *could not* set a New Year's resolution to lose x number of pounds. Here's where it got confusing though: it's not that I was not allowed to lose weight at all, because I was allowed to change my habits, exercise, treat my body better, and eat well to heal myself. Doing these things could very well result in weight loss. And that would be okay.

Secret Donuts

The instruction, however, was a wakeup call to the fact that for so long, I had been focusing on my weight and desiring weight loss with all my heart, mind, soul, and spirit for what I believed it would mean if I achieved it. The fact of the matter is that for too long, I had put my faith and hope in weight loss, and God was *tired* of it. Essentially, weight loss had become my idol. If you know God, then you know how he feels about idols. Yikes.

For as long as I can remember, my internal narrative has been "When I lose these 80 pounds:

I'm going to be poppin'.
I'm going to be a problem.
I'm going to finally go shopping.
I'm going the be the trophy wife my husband deserves.
I'm going to go get professional pictures taken.
I'm going to get in the picture with my kids.
I'm going to record those videos.
I'm going to brand myself.
I'm going to market my business.
I'm going to show up.
I'm going to start acting again.
I'm going to speak on stages.
I'm going to be ready."

I've come to realize that I had been conditioned to believe that I don't deserve to enjoy any of those things in my current state. And that's just not true. It's not true for me, and it's not true for you. It's time to call the enemy on his lies, and this book is where I am starting.

The journey to losing weight has to be preceded by a mindset shift. This mindset shift is a prerequisite. Much like the entry-level classes that you have to take in college in order to qualify for more advanced courses that have meat and substance, we have to lay a solid foundation of mind-rightness before body-snatchedness.

For God's babies (us), that's not just public declarations of body positivity, either. It's a foundational understanding that He loves us just as we are and expects us to as well. That's the destination we're aiming to reach.

So, if you're like me and you've been:

- looking at other people who have lost weight and secretly feeling envious or frustrated and upset with them because they were able to accomplish something that seemingly eludes you;
- feeling like your worth is attached to a number on the scale;
- feeling like you have no self-control over your diet and/or exercise; or
- having trouble getting over your weight and into your purpose;

then let's journey together.
No more secrets. No more shame.

PART I
Maybe You're Like Me
(My Story)

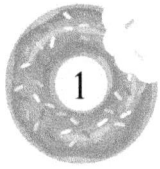

How Did I Get Here?

My backstory could take up the whole book, but seriously, this isn't a memoir. Nevertheless, I want to share my history with you because I want you to understand how deep it goes for me. Whenever I set out to lose weight, it's not simply discipline, determination, and "calories in and calories out." While that works for a lot of people, it doesn't work for me. I have a feeling that it hasn't worked for you, either. I want to share my story first to connect with you. To assure you that it's not only you. I want to show how far I've come so that you can see how powerful God is and hope and believe that He can do the same for you.

There are a few memories on the timeline of my existence that really illustrate how being obsessed with my weight has held such a prominent space in my mind and life. It has driven my actions, shaped my self-perception, and chipped away at my self-esteem and self-worth. I'll delve more deeply into how this has affected very important relationships in my life in detail later, but for now, here's a brief synopsis of how I got here.

***

"I'm going to the store. Do you want anything?"

"A honey bun."

I'd have this exact conversation with my mother nearly every day. Sweet, soft, squishy, and delicious, my love for donuts, brownies, cakes, and cookies started early, at about six years old. Maybe even earlier. I can't remember.

I do remember weighing 86 pounds in the third grade. Why do I remember that? Because when I told my aunt, she dramatically repeated it in disbelief and said that she, a grown woman, only weighed 120 pounds. Up until that point, I hadn't really understood the significance we place on a number on the scale. I learned quickly, though.

I remember weighing 139 pounds in sixth grade. Why? Because of the shame I felt having straight As on my report card but refusing to show it to my classmate to prove it because there, right next to my name, was my weight (for some strange, stupid, reason).

I weighed 190 pounds in eighth grade. I remember because I wore these ballooning white pants from the old ladies section of JC Penney's. That was the only place in the store that carried my size. I remember the day my parents bought them. That day, my quick-tempered father, who, like most men, would rather not spend an afternoon clothes shopping, exploded and stormed off somewhere. He got mad because of my whining and complaining about not being able to find anything that fit me. Later, he shared that on that day, he left us to find a place to cry. Y'all, up until that point, I'd seen my dad cry maybe two times in my entire life.

That's how helpless he felt for me. My parents never had to worry about their weight. They were both naturally thin, so they never had to watch what they ate in fear of packing on pounds. My brother was also naturally thin. That created a void in the way they nurtured me. I ate all of the junk, all of the snacks, all of the sweets, and none of the veggies and drank zero water. I'm not entirely sure if a diet and lifestyle change for me ever crossed their minds as something they had the power to enforce. On the other hand, they might have thought about it but felt like most of us parents feel: we don't want our kids to think that they are being punished for who and how they are. So, we accept them just as they are.

As a mother myself now, I become more aware every day of just how young my parents were when they had my brother and me. They were in a different position, a different frame of mind. Barely adults themselves and not having worked out their own issues and insecurities, they may not have had the mental space to deal with my issues. Later it occurred to me that as my mom went to that corner store and fed her addiction, she fed mine. Even as that was the case, through their hard work, love, and perseverance, they set me up to live a life where I can be in *this* mental space, to address the issue on my own. So I don't place blame on them. I gratefully stand on their shoulders, acknowledging the sacrifices they made to position me higher and to have less worry and strife than they had to endure.

As a kid, though, you look to adults to tell you who you are. I learned that I was smart, sweet, responsible, *good*, and well liked by adults. I'm an introvert by nature. Clinging to only a few friends, I wasn't the popular kid on the playground playing hand games, double-dutch, and hopscotch. I was the kid who stayed inside at recess helping my teacher by grading papers with the answer key and doing other tasks. These were definitions of myself that I could hold on to; things that made me special. But since the other kids didn't think so, there was still a part of me that desired to be pretty and popular. To at the very least be acknowledged by my crushes. That never happened.

Well, it happened once when I was in the sixth grade. Both sixth grade classes were invited to an end-of-the-year pool party. I was excited because swimming was one of my favorite things to do. My crush at the time was a Jonathan Taylor Thomas clone, down to his mischievous ways. He happened to look up at the moment I did the super-fast towel drop at the edge of the pool so that no one would catch a glimpse of me in my swimsuit thing. He caught a glimpse and promptly yelled out, "Watch out, everybody! Free Willy is going to squish you!" And everyone got as far away from me as they could, screaming and laughing.

That hurt.

Speaking of hurt, that brings to mind eighth grade. A friend of my crush at that time decided to prank him. He came to me and told me that my crush was crushing on me. Thinking it was a love match, I wrote a letter to him. Between those college-ruled faded blue lines I poured my little heart out. I caught him just before he got on his afternoon bus and handed him the letter with a smile on my face and a twinkle in my eye. It was a breezy spring day. The dappled sunlight shone through the fresh new leaves of this bright new season and warmed my cheeks almost to the temperature of my beating heart. As I stood there watching him get to his seat and open my letter, I waited for our eyes to lock so that I could blow him a kiss.

That didn't happen.

As the bus began to ease off of the curb, my crush opened the window and tossed my letter out of it. I watched in horror as it was carried off by that same wonderful spring breeze. Our eyes locked. He gave me the finger. The roar of laughter from the bus only grew fainter as it picked up speed and got further away.

The middle school years are trash.

In high school, I became active in sports and lost weight in a short amount of time. I was doing something I loved: cheerleading. I got down to about 150 pounds by the time I was 15. With my tallish 5'7" frame, I wasn't a stick, but I wasn't "fat" either. I was what people called "thick"— mostly toned and pretty fit. And still very unhappy.

I remember when my cousin (who's four years younger) came to visit from Maryland that summer. I broke down and cried because she was wearing a training bra. Why? Because I felt it was unfair that she was able to develop boobs. As a fat kid, I had "boobs" by fourth grade. I also had a belly, arms, legs, and chins, so seeing her made me feel like I was robbed of that milestone and rite of passage to womanhood.

On the other hand, I learned that "thick" was good. Boys started gassing me up, so I started feeling myself. I became a bit of a mean girl. I was a cheer captain dating the quarterback, getting the grades, and experiencing all the fun (and drama) that came with being in the popular crowd. I remember giggling and calling a girl "a fatback" because I didn't like that she had a crush on "my man." I didn't have a fat back anymore, so it was fine. I had joined the ranks of "them"—the ones I had admired for so long. The ones who seemed so happy. The ones who seemed so important to people they didn't even bother to see. The girls who were cute and could justifiably make fun of the not-so-cute girls. I was on the other side of the ugly stick, living the life I had always imagined. But honestly, I was fronting. I feigned confidence, while deep inside, I was still sad because my friends could wear single digits and I was still a size 10/12. I was smaller but still bigger than most of them. It wasn't enough.

The attention became addictive, and I sought attention. I acted the way they say girls who don't have a father in the home act. My dad had always been there, had always adored me, and had always expressed that. But I didn't want to be his type of beautiful. I wanted to be desired, and I wanted to be affirmed in my beauty. Couple that with teenage hormones, and I became boy crazy. Their words gave me confidence.

Their lustful glances stroked my ego. Their attention made me feel valued. But I hadn't learned my worth. I entertained too many conversations, too much flattery. And while I wasn't promiscuous, it at times appeared that I was. God's grace covered me in many situations that could have gone so far left because my "No" came so late during dates. I was still a "good" girl after all. I just lacked the common sense, street smarts, and people skills that my newfound friends had cultivated outside on playgrounds while I was inside clapping chalkboard erasers with my teacher pals.

By Thanksgiving break of my freshman year of college, I'd gained my freshman 10+. By the end of the academic year, I had gained 20+ pounds altogether. I remember my best friend calling me up and saying, "Someone asked me 'Where's Alicia? I haven't seen her around,'" to which she replied, "She's hiding."

Best friends know you best, huh? I really was hiding. I'd "fallen off," and I didn't want people to see me like that.

Throughout college, my confidence continued to be shaken up on a massive scale. Everything that I thought had made me special before, like being smart and pretty, no longer mattered because I had come to the land of smarter and prettier girls. And for a young woman who only valued herself when others valued her, that was detrimental. School was more challenging than I had ever experienced. The other women were gorgeous, dynamic, and confident (and we outnumbered the guys, so they could be choosey). Unfortunately, I was competitive in more than just sports. I would sit around a room of my friends, mentally ranking us, silently hating: "She's got a great shape, but her face?" My insecurities were blaring.

I spent the majority of my college years trying to get that old thing back—that thing that I had had in high school. I joined and later became the captain of a recreational dance team on campus. We performed and practiced regularly, but it wasn't as strenuous as my cheer team in high school. It was enough to maintain my weight, but I definitely wasn't losing anything since I also had a terrible diet. Outside of that, I worked out off and on but could never motivate myself enough to stay consistent.

Meanwhile, I reverted to shrinking in other ways. I became quieter, less noticeable, and more agreeable. I'm sweet by nature, but in order to be more likeable, I trained myself from a young age to make people feel good about me by being nice, smiling a lot, laughing at jokes that weren't funny, and putting other people's needs and desires before my own. I started to try to find my value through performance again, adding more and more activities to my plate. I'd lost a lot of my personality, my spunk, and my jubilance. I started to play the role of the stereotypical sitcom best friend—the occasionally funny, chubby girl who was there to support the ambitions and storyline of the cute popular star. I reverted to being the tag-along. I reverted to believing the lie that if I wasn't the prettiest, I didn't deserve to be the center of attention and I shouldn't draw attention to myself.

Secret Donuts

After college, I still struggled with my weight and confidence as I entered the workforce. I moved to the Washington, DC area for work and decided to pursue acting in my spare time. Talented as I was, I never had the confidence to go at it wholeheartedly, because while I played the stereotypical bff role in real life, I wanted to be the leading lady in my acting career. I never felt like I had "the look" though.

In 2007, I did a spiritual fast with my church and lost a significant amount of weight around the time I met my husband. I had gained most of it back by the time we got married two years later. Two months after that, I found out I was pregnant with our first child. To my absolute horror, I gained 80 pounds that *did not* come off with breastfeeding like the books and blogs had promised me.

Before the start of our second pregnancy a little over a year later, I managed to get off 20 of those pounds but gained about 40 through the pregnancy. That put me right back where I started. Since then, I've been burdened with two concurrent feelings: of the unfairness of life and of a secret disdain for women who were able to simply snapback to their pre-pregnancy weight. Again, my insecurities were running the show.

In the years that have followed, I've accomplished a lot on my own and with my family. But all the wins have been overshadowed in my mind by the need to lose weight. I often hide behind my husband's awesomeness and my kids' talents and cuteness. I've been pushing them into the spotlight, playing the backup dancer even though I know that our family is called and purposed to be a group act. Of that, I am certain.

There is so much irony in getting bigger physically and attempting to appear smaller in all other areas. Almost subconsciously, I've embraced not showing up and not drawing too much attention to myself. I'm almost embarrassed to say that my reasoning has been that I didn't want to be looked at as someone who had the audacity to accomplish things and to be present and visible when I wasn't snatched or looking amazing. Like, how dare I? The truth of the matter is, a lot of people equate fatness to laziness and insignificance. I'm guilty of it, too. But that's the very line of thinking that has kept me stuck not living up to my greatest potential. Perhaps you can relate? Perhaps you ask yourself far too often, "Who do I think I am?" or "Why would they listen to me?"

Working as a cinematographer and photographer has hipped me to another truth: we definitely judge ourselves far more harshly than others do. Nearly everyone I've worked with (mostly women) has received my finished product and complimented me on my technical expertise or artistry or creativity right before making a negative comment about her own appearance. Some things I have heard (and even said to my own photographer about myself—I'm guilty, too):

My arms look so big.

My skin looks bad.

I shouldn't have smiled at all. Smiling makes my face look fat.

Secret Donuts

I'm coming back to you when I lose weight.

I should have sucked in more.

Can you remove my double chin?

Don't get me wrong; I totally understand wanting to look your best—especially for images that will be available for a long, long while and have the potential to spread far and wide. But there's a difference between photoshopping flyaways or cleaning up some blemishes and photoshopping women's bodies until they're virtually unrecognizable. Somehow that's become the expectation: this pretend perfection. That's a setup and partially the reason why we are how we are as a culture today. But I'll get more into that later.

I'm perfectly suited for this kind of work. I'm a textbook empath. As a child, I had to kiss every stuffed animal I had goodnight and then explain to them all why I only slept with one bear in my bed. I didn't want anyone to feel less important than the others. My brother and father would harass me by punching my dolls and stuffed animals across the room while they cackled. I would cry because it was just so mean and I could feel their pain. When I was in high school, my parents and I were driving back home from a summer program I'd completed at Michigan State University. I broke down crying because there were so many dead deer lining the shoulder of the highway. I hate suffering of any kind for everyone. While I know that I am a talented artist and a gifted creative, I know that one of the main underlying reasons God put me in this position was to encourage, uplift, and champion his daughters. They suffer from the mental exhaustion of trying to live up to and maintain this distorted, impossible view of perfection. That's just not His will. Since He knows I despise liars and hypocrites and even more, that I don't want to be one, anything that I say to these ladies is also something that I can, should, and must say to myself. It's also evidence that I know better when I fall into that same kind of thinking. I have His Word and the power to speak life and truth over myself, too. And the reality is that whenever someone else views my work, they never pay attention to or comment on my clients' flaws. If they happen to notice, they don't dwell because the message and the intent behind the photos or videos are just that much more important. Those flaws don't stop them from experiencing the purpose we set out to accomplish with the project.

MESSAGE

For the people in the back who didn't catch it: your flaws can't stop your purpose from progressing. But you can if you allow your flaws to be an insurmountable obstacle.

For the longest time, I believed that carrying extra weight and not having an ideal body type were the missing elements to my awesomeness and success. Is that true for you, too? Do you find yourself getting hyped up about your gifts and talents, brilliance, and character only to, in the same breath, burst your own confidence bubble with negative thoughts about how fat you are? Do you watch other women do what you do (or what you want to do) on a level that you know that you are called to do in a way that you are capable of doing it and feel like they deserve the success but you don't because they are thin and you're not? I know the feeling. I can think of one person in particular. Our lives so closely mirrored each other's, it was nearly unbelievable (except that she had a teeny tiny little waist and a whole lot of confidence). We could have been great colleagues or collaborators, but my insecurities turned into hatred and bitterness, and I ended up obsessing over and talking about her every chance I got. And she gave plenty of chances, because she was showing up and being awesome. She was getting applause and recognition. She was enjoying the spoils of her hard work, but all I could see was the unfairness of her having that little bitty waist and banging body which, in my mind, were *clearly* the reasons she was winning.

I'm so very shallow. We're all so very shallow. As a society, a culture, and a human race, we've valued beauty above all throughout history. I'm truly glad God doesn't look at the same things that we look at when He's looking for someone to use to do His work. For instance, in 1 Samuel 16, God sends Samuel to Jesse's house to anoint one of his sons as the new King of Israel. Samuel arrives prepared to anoint only the very best, but his criteria for a king were quickly dismantled by God.

"When they came, he looked on Eliab and thought, 'Surely the Lord's anointed is before him.' But the Lord said to Samuel, 'Do not look on his appearance or on the height of his stature, because I have rejected him. **For the Lord sees not as man sees: man looks on the outward appearance, but the Lord looks on the heart**'" (1 Samuel 16: 6-7 NLT, emphasis my own).

Maybe it's worth considering that what's on the inside of us is far more valuable to God and to the world than our outward appearance. Yes, the world might value what we look like more, but what they actually need is what we carry on the inside: our substance, our character, our gifts and talents. Might it be worth considering that if we got on the same wavelength as God on this, then we would be able to accept that regardless of what we look like, when we open our hearts and look more like Jesus, there is no greater beauty?

I've come to accept that being overweight is an ever-present reminder of my imperfection but also an ever-present reminder of God's infinite wisdom. I've overlooked my internal beauty for far too long. I thought of it as of no consequence, giving it the background, denying who God said I am because I don't yet look like I think I should. But what I have learned is that until I get my view of myself in alignment with God's view of me, I won't be successful in fulfilling my purpose and calling. I won't be able to live peacefully without inner turmoil and with contentment.

I've spent so much time trying to get myself qualified through achieving a banging body to add to all of my other great qualities with which I've been blessed. However, God does not call the qualified; he qualifies the called. If I gave just 75 percent of the energy that I spend on trying to figure out how to lose weight to the things that I know that I'm supposed to be doing at the time, how much more powerful and effective might I be for Kingdom work? Maybe, just maybe, if I were to just focus on my calling and on God's people and their needs, then I would eventually get to the space where He could get me in shape physically, emotionally, spiritually, and mentally. I know that this is my backstory, but I have a feeling that this is true for you, too.

I find affirmation of this in Matthew 6:33: "But seek first his kingdom and his righteousness, and all these things will be given to you as well" (NIV).

"These things" refer to the things that God knows we need, yet we needlessly worry about. "These things" are important, but they are not the most important. Yes, I still plan to lose the weight eventually. But consider this: if you're like me, you can't work or live in clutter (no matter how hard you try). You'll open your laptop, look up, and see that the dishes need to be done, and next thing you know, you're busting suds. I can't really function when things are out of order. So then it makes sense that I haven't been able to get my life together in this area because "weight loss over everything" is so out of order.

Throughout my adult years, I have come to understand that food is my struggle area. I don't mind working out. There were many seasons in which I was consistently physically active, utilizing my gyms and physical training resources at work. But the saying is true: you can't outwork a bad diet. I visited a nutritionist while in college. As she started to give me advice, I found myself finishing her sentences. Finally she asked me, "Why are you here? You already know everything you need to know." She wasn't being facetious; she was genuinely curious. And she was right. I knew *what* to do.

What I needed to learn was *why* I couldn't and wouldn't just do it. About five or six years ago, I looked up Overeaters Anonymous. On their website, they had a questionnaire designed to determine if you have a problem with compulsive eating. I cried while reading those questions, because it felt like each and every one of them was describing my struggles. I took down the information to go to a meeting but never went.

I think I knew deep down inside that overeating wasn't the diagnosis but a symptom. Something deeper was driving this. Later, I'd realize that if I wanted to have lasting and meaningful change in my physical actions, I'd have to first address what was going on in my soul and spirit. With that in mind, in October of 2016, I finally started therapy.

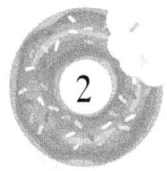

How Do I Get Out of Here?

"But when you open your mouth!" my therapist passionately, almost pleadingly interrupted me. Her tone pierced me, alerted me to reality as if I kept missing it—because I did.

A few seconds before, I was sharing that I was feeling some anxiety about meeting some people with whom my husband had been working for months. They were producing a stage play that we wrote together on a scale that he and I had yet to be able to produce in the three years we'd been presenting it.

It was an amazing opportunity and a fantastic blessing, and while I had been very hands on in past runs of the play, this time I sat it out, gleefully watching and cheering from the sidelines. I was busy taking care of home, the kids, and my video production company.

Then came the request: would I mind filming and editing a few scenes? Of course I wouldn't! I set to work on reading the script again, storyboarding, creating my shot list, and preparing myself to do one of my favorite things to do ever. However, reality set in as the shoot day approached. I started to think about their reactions to me: the other name in the written byline that they might have heard so much about. I imagined that they would see me and with utter disappointment say, "Oh, that's his wife?"

"But when you open your mouth!"

"Yeah…" I politely, half-heartedly agreed with a half-smile.

She continued. She spoke of my gifts and talents, of my vision, of my heart, of my empathy, and of my creativity. She spoke of how many people I would touch and help in the future. She kept pouring into me. Kept uplifting. Kept speaking the truth as she saw it—as someone quite literally on the outside looking in because I allowed her into that space. And thank God that I did. That day I wasn't exactly convinced as we continued on with our session, but even now it still resonates. The statement replays in my head when I start to place too much weight on my weight.

I have been overweight for over 25 years of my life. The number on the scale has gone up and down and in each direction has taken my confidence with it. The overcompensation for being a fat kid in a family of skinny people started early. I excelled academically and placed all of my ego eggs in the basket of accomplishment. When you become an adult, however, they stop handing out grades, ribbons, and trophies. The closest you're going to get are your performance reviews at work.

You can imagine, then, the confusion spiral I went down when I decided to leave my job and run my company full time. There was no one there to pat me on the back. There was no one there to tell me I'm doing great or to say I'm the best. No set, consistent salary to validate my capabilities. I came face to face with a huge revelation: I need to learn to just *be* and allow that to be enough. It would have to be enough to show up (and confidently at that). I would have to be grateful for and take pride in the simple fact that I exist and have unique traits within me that are worth celebrating and sharing. Against what seemed to be instinct, I've had to actively agree with the notion that my worth and value in this world are not dependent upon the number on my clothes tags or the number on my scale.

Because that's what we've been taught, right? "Fat people are lazy. Fat people lack self-control. Fat people have low self-worth, and they absolutely should because they are fat and are worth less." We praise women who snap back immediately after the bodily trauma of pregnancy and childbirth. We live in the gym. We watch what we eat and deny ourselves. A lot of times it's not out of concern for our health and in honor of our temples but to avoid the guilt of shame that comes with the headshakes and whispers of "Yikes, she really let herself go."

That therapy session was my wakeup call. Too often I operate from a space of deficit, focusing on what I don't have instead of celebrating, then utilizing, what I do. What my therapist helped me to understand was that even if I didn't show up looking like a trophy wife (by my own impossible standards, mind you), what happens when I open my mouth and share what I have inside is reason enough to show up fully and allow God to use this imperfect vessel. In that way, He can receive all of the glory because (not in spite) of my physical imperfection. I had to start seeing this burden of being overweight as a catalyst for connection instead of a cause for condemnation.

I didn't get this way overnight, neither mentally nor physically, so the work I am putting in to change my mindset and to care for my temple from a space of love for who I am and not out of shame of what I am not is ongoing. I am reminded of when Jesus went into the wilderness to be tempted by Satan. There in that desolate, vulnerable place, Satan told Jesus lies that sounded like truth, lies that Satan even twisted around and supported with scripture. But prior to that encounter, Jesus studied, learned, and knew enough for himself to discount even the most believable lies. He knew who He was, whose He was, and most importantly, what that meant.

The Devil really is a liar. He's been whispering lies to me since I was eight years old, when I first gained weight, just so that he can manifest and keep me bound up for such a time as this. But no more. With each step on my journey, the narrative I entertain, believe, and repeat about myself changes more and more. It sounds more like truth. It sounds more like love. It sounds more like God.

I've opened my mouth.

Can't Serve Both God and...

Okay. I'm going to be real and just say it: weight loss has been an idol for me. Does that mean I worship at the altar of the god of thigh gaps (is that even a thing)? No, but what it looks like is me putting all of my trust, hope, and faith in losing weight and being the perfect size and shape. For as long as I can remember, I've been wanting, praising, and seeking weight loss for what I've felt like it could do for my life. I've believed that losing weight would make people respect me, that it would open more doors to success, that I would finally be worthy of and secure in my relationships (romantic and platonic). Young girls could finally look up to me. I'd conquer my self-control issues. My husband could finally cherish me again. I would finally be significant enough. I would finally have it *all* together.

I've been treating weight loss like it's a god. And I have a feeling I'm not the only one.

We're not in the Bible days, so sometimes it's harder to spot idolatry. We are not physically building golden calves or wooden poles to dance around and make burnt offerings.

But we can build something up so much in our minds and hearts that we pursue it relentlessly with the same zeal and fervor with which we should be pursuing God. An idol can be anything from a relationship, to money, to success, to a prestigious job. It's anything that we rank up above God in order of importance. Or worse, we try to use God to obtain that thing. We might try to make Him serve it. We can believe He's able to give it to us and resent Him if He doesn't. If the only time you are going to God in prayer is to be blessed with that thing you hope for and desire, then you might be making an idol of it.

I love God deeply, but I definitely, absolutely did this with weight loss. If you could read my prayer journals, you'd find that 75 percent of their content over the years has been devoted to asking God to show me how to lose weight, asking God for forgiveness for not losing weight, asking God to whoosh the weight away, crying out to God because I'm sick of being overweight, questioning God for making me overweight, and so on. I have sought it out, read up on it, looked for the best ways to achieve it, and sought out other people's testimonies and transformations as motivation. These are not bad things at all in the proper context. But for me, weight loss has been a barrier to obedience. Weight loss has dominated my thoughts, and I've been subconsciously trying to use God as just one more way to solve the problem. That makes it problematic.

These days, it's like a badge of honor to eat right and exercise. And don't get me wrong, having self-control and exercising self-care is very important and absolutely commendable. But as daughters of God, you should not be more comfortable talking about weight loss than you do about the Gospel. You should not find yourself thinking more about weight loss than you do the Kingdom of God.

I did though. And coming into 2018, God called me out on it. As clear as day, I heard from him that I was making weight loss my god, and God don't play that. And yep, that revelation bopped me over the head just like Homey D. Clown did the little kids with his little sock weapon. You can be devoted to God, living out your purpose, trying to be a good person, repenting for your sins, serving His people, and still miss it if your heart is out of order. My heart was out of order.

Even while believing that weight loss would make me happy, making weight loss an idol has actually made me miserable. Hope deferred makes the heart sick, and I put off life and all its fullness while putting my hope and faith in getting thinner. This is the main problem: weight loss has been an all-or-nothing concept to me. Without it, none of my other qualities, achievements or blessings mattered, but with it my life would finally be perfect.

Oh that elusive p word: perfection. Somehow we've tricked ourselves into thinking that perfection exists. And with the help of social media, we're being tricked into thinking other people's lives are perfect. They're not. They are, however, telling a perfect story, shaping a perfect image, and sometimes being perfectly dishonest (all in the hopes of gaining financial or social capital). Meanwhile, we're scrolling by believing and double-tapping the limited information that they are presenting. We find ourselves comparing it with the totality of our real lives—with all its ups and downs, wins and losses. No wonder we are miserable. No wonder we are striving. No wonder we're upset and frustrated. A chasing after the wind like Solomon. A punching of the air like Cuba Gooding Jr. in *Boyz in the Hood*.

We have to chill.

I've spent so long in a prison of my own making, bound up by a desire for perfection that is not only impossible but unnecessary. I've been striving to be the total package without acknowledging that that leaves no room for God. Perfect people don't need God. I do. Do you?

It brings me back to Matthew 6:33 and how I've been out of order. My thought process was that once I lost the weight I would be better suited to serve God, not realizing the pursuit of weight loss first was the thing that was putting a rift in between us. A few verses earlier in Matthew 6:24 (NLT), Jesus tells us, "No one can serve two masters. Either you will hate the one and love the other, or you will be devoted to the one and despise the other. You cannot serve both God and money." In this case, I could not serve both God and weight loss. And that was becoming more and more apparent. Some days, I'd find myself so fed up that I would literally cry out and plead with God to let this "cup" pass. Then I would be frustrated with Him when in the morning I walked past my bathroom mirror only to find that I hadn't miraculously dropped 80 pounds overnight. I became more and more disgruntled when I thought of how unfair it was that I've spent the majority of my life being "big boned" and just a Big Mac away from blowing up. Why would God withhold this from me? Why would He make me this way?

Perfection is a myth. Believing that losing weight was the key to my life being perfect was misguided and simply not true. Because realistically, what being overweight has really been is a thorn. Let's look at 2 Corinthians 12:6 to see what I mean:

"Therefore, in order to keep me from becoming conceited, I was given a thorn in my flesh, a messenger of Satan, to torment me. **Three times I pleaded with the Lord to take it away from me. But he said to me, 'My grace is sufficient for you, for my power is made perfect in weakness.'** Therefore I will boast all the more gladly about my weaknesses, so that Christ's power may rest on me. That is why, for Christ's sake, I delight in weaknesses, in insults, in hardships, in persecutions, in difficulties. For when I am weak, then I am strong" (NLT, emphasis my own).

Thorns are annoying, prickly, and painful at times, but they often protect something beautiful. His grace is that beautiful thing for me. The thorn is the thing that brings me back to God to show me that His grace is enough. Beyond what the world thinks and says and beyond what they reward, the things that I receive and the doors that are opened to me are and have always been because of His grace. I have received them because of how He formed me—just the way

He wanted to. Throughout this journey, I've been leaning on the word of David in Psalm 139, especially verses 13-16 (NLT):

> "You made all the delicate, inner parts of my body
> and knit me together in my mother's womb.
> Thank you for making me so wonderfully complex!
> Your workmanship is marvelous—how well I know it.
> You watched me as I was being formed in utter seclusion,
> as I was woven together in the dark of the womb.
> You saw me before I was born.
> Every day of my life was recorded in your book.
> Every moment was laid out
> before a single day had passed."

If I believe God's Word, and these words specifically, then I have no choice but to accept that God did, in fact, make me this way on purpose. And He made me this way for His purpose. It's not a mistake or coincidence that this is my struggle. Looking at it from this point of view enables me to embrace that this struggle is not something that keeps me from being amazing. Instead, it works in tandem with all of my other amazing qualities that He uniquely placed within me. Through my empathy, I can feel and relate to others who share this struggle or whatever struggle they have. Through my humility, gentleness, and compassion, I can uplift and celebrate all shapes and sizes. As a countercultural, world-changing artist, I can convey these feelings in truth and also break stereotypes with conviction through my work. As an intentional mother, I can shape and mold my children to see people as God sees them. And as a dynamic writer, I'm able to write this book with the transparency and vulnerability that will help me to connect with sisters who silently share the burden of being bound up by shame and perfectionism. These, His daughters, with whom He seeks to have a word, through me nonetheless! This thing that I have perceived for so long to be a flaw is actually a vessel and a blessing. Amen.

For years I worked as an adjudicator for the government. My responsibilities included deciding who was worthy of a security clearance and having access to our nation's secrets. We gave access based on the totality of a person's life. One achievement didn't qualify a person to receive a security clearance just as one bad decision didn't always disqualify him. We used all of the information we had at hand to help us to understand a person's character. It's so funny that I studied, was a distinguished graduate of our training, was credentialed, and worked for several years doing that work, but was unable to see the connection. I couldn't see that I needed to apply the same whole person concept to my perception of myself. For many years, I have not given myself clearance to show up and do all that I have been placed here to do because I judged myself on one area of my life. No matter how much everything else has pointed to my having a good character, I've let this one area disqualify me in my own mind.

I've been missing it.

This skewed perception of weight is why in this season of my life, I agree with God that it is necessary to delay my weight loss journey. Maybe you need to, too. When I tell people about it, I am met with looks of confusion. And I get it. It's not something you typically hear. It doesn't sound wise or conventional to not want to immediately lose weight and become your "best self." I assume that people silently judge me because it seems like I let myself go, and from the sound of it, now I'm totally giving up and giving in. It might sound like I've become complacent. I've found this to be true: when you're seeking to grow personally, not everyone will be on board with your method or your process. Many people won't welcome that change in action or the shift in perspective. And many people won't understand or support it. But it's not for or about them. This is between me and God. This is between *you* and God.

Ultimately, we need to realistically redefine weight for ourselves. We have to remix the negative tape that replays in our minds. We need to separate our weight from our identity. We need to separate it from others' identities. We need to retrain our minds to not hinge anybody's worth on how much they weigh, how fit they are, or how sexy they look.

If I'm being honest, I'm not even in the space where I don't want to lose weight. I do. Listen, I would really like to lose weight. But there is work to be done first in my mind so that I don't continue to seek to lose weight for all the wrong reasons. Additionally, I have to do the mental work so that my perspective doesn't swing from one extreme to another, namely body positivity (for the sake of body positivity or political correctness). I want to love and cherish my body, yes, but not *solely* as an act of rebellion against societal norms and definitely not at the expense of my overall health.

Romans 12:2 (NLT) reminds us: "Don't copy the behavior and customs of this world, but let God transform you into a new person by changing the way you think. Then you will learn to know God's will for you, which is good and pleasing and perfect."

I want to depend on Christ to help me make that mental shift. I desire for my body positive mindset to come from a space of authenticity and truth because realistically, I don't and I can't love this body (in all of its forms) apart from Christ. I've been through too much in my life to be able to force myself into a different way of thinking. I need the renewing power of the Holy Spirit to guide me into a new mental space and appreciation.

While I do believe I am attractive, I know that beauty is fleeting and charm is deceptive, but a woman who loves the Lord is to be praised. That love for the Lord makes me so much more dynamic as a whole person than my looks alone ever will. I can lose my looks, I can lose favor with people, but my love for God and my obedience to Him are things that I have control over. And they are far more richly rewarded than just being a trophy wife or being well-loved or being accomplished and successful. But again, in the right order, I can have all of these things plus peace. So no, at this point, I don't have a problem with delaying weight loss, because by obsessing over it, I've been delaying the abundance of life that Jesus has promised me. And beyond that, as if I needed any more motivation to change, I've come to realize that this quest for weight loss has negatively affected so many other people in many areas of my life. Most concerning are the very specific areas I have been called to purposely serve, namely: my marriage, my children, and my business. In the next few sections, I will share exactly how.

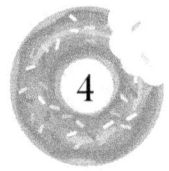

We Need to Make a U-Turn

FOR RICHER OR POORER; THROUGH BACK-ROLLS AND SNATCHED-WAISTEDNESS

Ray grabbed my phone out of my hand and held it high above his head out of my reach.

"Who is 'him'?"

I giggled and screamed that he needed to give me my phone back.

"Who is 'him'?" He asked in a more demanding tone, now grinning and effortlessly fanning away my attempts at my phone.

Flashback to a few minutes before. I had just tried to remind him of when we were at the store and I had bought a particular shirt, but I stopped abruptly and said, "Oh, that wasn't you."

What I meant was that he wasn't there; that I was shopping alone.

He hit me with, "If it wasn't me, then who was it?" to which I flippantly replied, "Him" as I started to scroll through social media. That's when he grabbed my phone and stood up on our bed.

The scene that played out after that was cute like a 90s rom-com. In the moment, we were like playful little teenagers—tickle fighting, wrestling, shadow boxing, and giggling uncontrollably. But because we are not teenagers, we tired out quickly. We both fell back onto the bed, breathing heavily, staring at the ceiling with smiles on our faces. My smile faded.

"You know there's no 'him.'"

"Better not be."

"Nobody else wants me."

Womp womp. Instant mood killer.

Then the monologue started in my mind, "How many times do I have to remind me that self-loathing isn't sexy?"

He said nothing in response. Silence is his safe-space in these instances (instances that I admit happen a little too often in our marriage). My usual reaction to the silence is frustration. In my mind, I think, "I'm pouring out my heart to you, letting you into a vulnerable, space and you *need* to build me up in it. You need to *affirm me*! Hello, hi. It's my love language. Do your job, sir."

I said that I said that in my mind. I'm lying. I've said that mess out loud (more than a couple of times). And my husband, being a man's man who seeks to solve problems, one time actually listened to me. By the next day, I had sticky notes hidden all over the house. What was on them? Affirmations and declarations of his love for me to discover.

Secret Donuts

And the crowd goes, "Awwwwww."

How did I react? "It's wonderful. Thank you. But I kinda meant I wanted it to be authentic and in the moment. Like when you are overwhelmed by my beauty, you say something right then or take pictures of me walking away or tell everybody how blessed you are to have me on your Facebook status. You know, stuff like that."

The man couldn't win. The "who is 'him'" incident happened well after "Operation Sticky Notes." And I still wasn't satisfied. I still wasn't convinced. Hence the silence. What was he supposed to say in that moment, though? Really, what? Because as history had taught us, if he had said anything affirming, I probably would not have believed it.

If I'm being honest, the problem isn't him. The problem is me. I complained that I wanted to hear affirmation. What I really wanted was confirmation. But confirmation is reinforcement of a belief. What I wanted to hear could not reinforce what I already believed about myself. What I *believed* about myself made anything he said a lie. Automatically. No matter how honest and sincere he was, I just couldn't receive it. He couldn't possibly believe I was sexy, desirable, and a wife he could be proud to have on his arm, because I didn't.

If I'm being even more honest, *that*, that mindset, has been more detrimental to our marriage than my inability to get the weight off. When you hold negative beliefs about yourself, then it's also easy to project them onto others. That projection had me living in an unspoken state of fear. I was constantly waiting for the other shoe to drop. Here I was with this handsome, extremely talented, amazing husband and father to my children, and in my mind, it was just a matter of time before he got bored with me and went out and found the beautiful, snatched-waisted woman he deserved. It was just a matter of time before the jig was up.

I became highly suspicious and territorial. I wanted to check his emails and social. I followed his gaze as we walked past pretty women. I wondered if he really went to the hardware store or just picked a location far away enough that I wouldn't question the time he was gone. I lived with dread. I was frustrated with myself. I felt helpless because I was racing against time to get the weight off to save a marriage that, in reality, was not in trouble.

How shallow and empty of a marriage we would have if that were all it was about: how sexy I was and how he got to brag about it at the water cooler or in a caption on social media? That seemed to be all I really wanted, though. I conveniently overlooked all that we truly have while focusing on what we don't. We truly are soulmates. We share the same values and interests. We work well together and have been building and creating art, both together and apart, since the beginning. I believe our marriage is purpose driven. Apart we're great, but together we're a force. Everything that we bring to the table as individuals completes the beautiful triangle between man, woman, and God that makes this marriage powerful and impactful. Not perfect. No one ever said it would be perfect. Yet here I was again, trying to achieve perfection (and suffering for it).

It's a very tone-deaf perspective to have in a relationship that I claimed I wanted to work. Embracing my feelings and projecting those feelings onto him left no room to acknowledge his feelings, let alone accept them. No one wants to be called a liar, least of all my husband. Integrity is a big deal to him. So if every time he compliments me I challenge him about whether he honestly feels that way or say something to the effect that he's just saying something to make me feel good, eventually it's bound to create a rift between us. There were days I would watch his jaws clench in frustration. On other days, his eyes would gloss over in despair and then defeat. I could see his wheels turning, trying to figure out how to convince me that he meant what he said. It was almost in vain though; unfortunately, he was trying to win an argument that I was essentially having with myself.

Insecurities are dangerous to a relationship. If you want a healthy relationship and if you want it to last, it's in your best interest to address them. There are two people in this marriage. We move as one, but both parties should be on the same page. At some point, I had to acknowledge that I was the problem, but not in the way that I thought I was. Not in the way that my insecurities said I was. I wasn't a victim who needed saving, but the heroine who needed to simply find the inner strength and determination to use all of the powers she had inside. I didn't need to take Ray's outstretched hand and try to pull him down into the pits with me, but take that hand and allow him to pull me up to stable ground. To stand securely in his love and God's love, at that moment, in the present. Not mentally fixing the past that had already ended or focusing on an uncontrollable future that hasn't begun. No, he needs me here and now, in whatever battle that's in front of us. He needs me to believe I'm a worthy companion just as much as he does.

It's important to determine a why in everything. Here's mine for my marriage: that we grow as individuals, as a couple, raise amazing children, and ultimately, that God gets all of the glory for and through it.

Earlier in 2018, I posted a picture on Instagram after a workout with a caption that said "Countdown to Costa Rica." At that moment, my eyes were opened. The clouds parted and I received a revelation. My husband truly loves me. Of course I had known that before, but I didn't know-know it. I didn't embrace it with my heart.

This trip to Costa Rica was significant because it was an all-expenses-paid vacation that we won because he entered an essay in a contest. That essay detailed our love and our marriage. I learned that not only was his entry selected but also that the essay was far more touching and beautiful than any of the other entries they received. I've never read the essay, but I believe every word of it.

What I've learned through this marriage is a concept that's sometimes still very hard to grasp and internalize. It's that my husband finds value in *me*; in me just being me. Somewhere along the line, I had internalized self-objectification. My value was wrapped up in how people felt about me and what I did for them, needing to be someone people bragged about and who made people want to count themselves as blessed simply because I was around. And when that wasn't happening, I began to feel mighty low.

But this love has been different. Throughout all of my outbursts and sorting things out, diets, and starts and stops with self-care, he has tried his best to love me fully and consistently as a husband and a brother in Christ. He has loved me with all the heart and soul he put behind his marriage vows. For richer or poorer; through back rolls and waist-snatchedness. Would he like me to be smaller and healthier? I'm sure he would. He wants me to look and feel my best—but for me. Because the thing that he has always found attractive is confidence. And ultimately the thing that he wants most for me is for me to be happy and at peace.

That's both confirming and affirming.

Knowing this gives me freedom to be confident and find value in who I am and not who I am perceived to be. His love encourages me to not look toward the shiny, glossy (realistically unpredictable) future, but to *live* fully in the here and now because it is just as beautiful, flaws and all. Because I am just as beautiful, flaws and all. Because if he can love me simply for me, who am I not to? That's what marriage is supposed to do, folks. It turns a mirror on you and forces you to see and fix your own issues (not your partner's). So, I've resolved to relieve him of the responsibility and pressure of building me up. I started therapy to work through the scars from my past and to reintroduce some mystery into our marriage. There are some things that I brought to my husband and some burdens that I placed on him that definitely were better suited for a mental health professional. Now I combine that with reading the Word, praying and journaling to battle the 25+ years of lies about myself that I've internalized. I'm intentional and I'm fighting because I am unwilling to sacrifice my marriage to the idol of weight loss, especially when the blessing I seek to receive in return is that same marriage. How asinine, right? Anway, 1 Corinthians 13:1 tells us all the things that love is. "Love is sexy" isn't one of them. I no longer want to be a trophy wife. I no longer feel the need to be. Healthy? Yes. Youthful, vibrant, confident, and pulled together? Absolutely, yes. But now I acknowledge that *this* man loves me beyond my face and beyond my body. Daily he looks down into the depths of me and sees worth. He looks at the totality of me and sees beauty. He desired me when I felt least desirable with a love that was independent of himself. In a word: unconditionally. That's the trophy. That's the prize.

LOVE IS THE GREATEST

13 If I could speak all the languages of earth and of angels, but didn't love others, I would only be a noisy gong or a clanging cymbal. 2 If I had the gift of prophecy, and if I understood all of God's secret plans and possessed all knowledge, and if I had such faith that I could move mountains, but didn't love others, I would be nothing.

3 If I gave everything I have to the poor and even sacrificed my body, I could boast about it but if I didn't love others, I would have gained nothing.

4 Love is patient and kind.
Love is not jealous or boastful or proud 5 or rude.
It does not demand its own way. It is not irritable, and it keeps no record of being wronged.
6 It does not rejoice about injustice but rejoices whenever the truth wins out.
7 Love never gives up, never loses faith, is always hopeful, and endures through every circumstance.
8 Prophecy and speaking in unknown languages and special knowledge will become useless. But love will last forever!
9 Now our knowledge is partial and incomplete, and even the gift of prophecy reveals only part of the whole picture!
10 But when the time of perfection comes, these partial things will become useless.
11 When I was a child, I spoke and thought and reasoned as a child. But when I grew up, I put away childish things.
12 Now we see things imperfectly, like puzzling reflections in a mirror, but then we will see everything with perfect clarity. All that I know now is partial and incomplete, but then I will know everything completely, just as God now knows me completely.
13 Three things will last forever—faith, hope, and love—and the greatest of these is love.
1 Corinthians 13:1-13 (NLT)

YO! WHO RAISED YOU PEOPLE? OH WAIT, I DID

As I was preparing breakfast for my kids one day, my daughter, who was five at the time, looked down and told me my tummy was too big. I asked her why, and she said it looked like I was having a baby. I asked her why that was a bad thing. Then my eight-year-old son chimed in saying that it was "just bad." I wouldn't back down, though. I needed answers. I really wanted them to tell me why they felt that way. I really wanted an in depth explanation. I challenged them to form words around this opinion they held.

That's a very different space for me to be in. A year before, heck, even a few months before, I would have had a different, more wounded response. With a veiled smile, I would have simply replied, "That's not nice, baby." My daughter is brutally honest. It's not the first time she has come for my weight.

But it was the first time that in one of those moments I felt a need to unteach them what I had to unlearn myself.

There's a scene in the movie *Mean Girls* where the popular girls are at Regina George's house. They all stand in front of the mirror, and three of them rattle off things they hate about themselves. Then they all look expectantly at Cady, who hadn't contributed to the conversation, and she says, "Oh…I have really bad breath in the morning." Cady hadn't learned the cultural practice of picking apart her physical appearance because she had grown up in Africa. But, here, in America, we learn to do it from a very young age.

Secret Donuts

Have your children ever heard you say, "I look so fat in this" or "Ew, look at my _____! I really hate it/them"? How many diets and/or new ways of eating has your daughter watched you start and stop? Or have you been like me and outright told your children, "Mommy needs to lose some weight"?

I cringe when I think about how many different ways I've demonstrated my displeasure with myself in front of my children, both verbally and nonverbally. Can you relate? What's more, I can even think back to times when I would watch a show or movie with them and be entertained when the fat character would do what fat characters stereotypically did. I wouldn't question it. It's just cultural. Just like being afraid of gaining weight is cultural and holding a negative opinion of someone who is overweight is cultural, we accept these points of view as normal because they have been normalized. But standing in the kitchen that day, it became glaringly apparent that normal does not equate to "right."

As mothers, is it is our responsibility to give our children opportunities to grow up and say, "Mama used to say…" The wisdom that we intentionally share with our children should be fruitful for their lives and the lives of anyone they touch and with whom they interact. My goal is to make sure that my children know their value and that they understand their identity and where it originates. I want them to be strong and proud and fully embrace who they are, because they were known before they were even formed in my womb.

In order to do that, I first had to evaluate those same traits within myself, because as *my* mama used to say, "I can show you better than I can tell you." Of course, I could tell them how they should feel, how they should act, and what they should or should not accept from other people. But if I myself was not modeling that for them, then I was at the very best a hypocrite and at the worst a liar. And my kids know how much I despise liars.

I also want my children to value other people, though. I want them to see people, to empathize with people, to love people, to serve people, and to treat people as they would themselves. Oh, I also want them to treat themselves like people. Don't you want the same for your children? In order for that to happen, we have to start with dismantling the micro-ideologies that they've been hearing and learning in places outside of our homes. We have to break down those ideals or at the very least make sure that our children know that they have the power to control that narrative for themselves. We have to give them the tools and the control to accept or deny the validity of those thoughts about other people. I can think of no better tool than the word of God.

As Romans 12:2 urges us, "Do not conform to the pattern of this world, but be transformed by the renewing of your mind. Then you will be able to test and approve what God's will is—his good, pleasing and perfect will" (NIV).

When I stand in my kitchen and my children tell me that I should not be fat, I'm going to call them on that. I plan to raise children who know how to think. I don't want them to be cultural sheep *or* religious fanatics. They should be able to articulate why they hold the views that they hold and defend those views with intelligent, well thought-out responses and with hearts that are pure toward others. I don't want them to tell people they shouldn't be fat just because they have received superficial messages from the world that "fat is bad." In fact, not too long ago, having extra fat was actually a symbol of wealth and affluence. The prosperous weren't affected by famine or food shortages, and it physically showed. Eventually, though, with changes to the food and agriculture industry, the beauty goal post moved, and being overweight became something to look down on. Beauty trends and standards are constantly changing. Look at a picture of your eyebrows from 1998 and call me a liar. Thankfully, our worth and value to God are the same yesterday, today, and forever. He wants us to see ourselves just as He does.

I want my children to always hold their opinions up to the Word of God to ensure that they align because God's word is also unchanging. That might seem farfetched for a five- and eight-year-old. That's fair. But at the very least, my job is to plant the seeds in their hearts to know to go in that direction when they are capable. Proverbs 22:6 reminds us to, "Start children off on the way they should go, and even when they are old they will not turn from it" (NIV).

That day in the kitchen, if they had looked at me and said, "Mommy, I'm not sure that you're healthy. I love you so much. I would like you to stay here with me for as long as possible and maybe even meet my children's children.

Please get in better shape," I would have been more willing to accept their concern. Again, at five and eight, that is not how that conversation would normally go down. But I don't want to raise normal children. I don't want to raise shallow children. I don't want to raise popular children. I don't even need to raise the best and the brightest children. I just want to raise content, confident, compassionate thought leaders who will become adults who do good and live out their God-given purpose from a space of conviction, security, truth, and authenticity.

That won't happen if I continue to live with an irrational fear of gaining weight or remaining overweight. Turning back to the Word, we find that such fear is unfounded. "For God has not given us a spirit of fear and timidity, but of power, love, and self-discipline." (2 Timothy 1:7, NLT). That kind of fear is a lie and comes straight from the enemy. How can I tell them to live boldly if I don't show them first?

Being a pseudo-millennial suburban mother is a curious thing. There are little expectations that I didn't know existed while growing up in the urban, inner-city southeast side of Grand Rapids, Michigan. Now that I'm here, one thing that I have found is that people love to send and receive unbasic Christmas cards. These are elaborate cards with pictures of their families on them. Some have little articles with updates on each family member's year. I think they are all fabulous. Ladies from my moms' groups schedule perfectly manicured family photo shoots months in advance. They scour the Internet for outfits that match and coordinate for their family. Then the cards are prepped, printed, and mailed by the time December rolls around. In the early days of my marriage, we received many, many Christmas cards in the mail. We've probably sent out one card total, and we're going on a decade of being married. We receive a lot fewer Christmas cards these days. I assume it's because people think that they were removed from our list, and in kind, they subsequently took us off of theirs. I totally get it, and I understand that postage stamps are not cheap; no hard feelings at all. But I want to take this moment to say this to all of my dear family and friends: you're still on the list.

I always have the best intentions going into the holiday season. I would schedule family shoots and then not be able to bring myself to plan for them. I would start to gather inspiration and outfit ideas and then chicken out because I didn't want to be photographed at all. Looking at inspiration picture after inspiration picture of families with fit, fabulous moms usually triggered me. By the time I'd pull the plug, it would be too late (and basically too basic) to send out standard cards without pictures. So, no one received any kind of card. And that became my pattern until I stopped trying altogether. Bah humbug.

Getting in the picture with my family has always been kind of a big deal. We've had two family pictures in all the time we've been married. The first one included my son when he was four months old. The second was when my son was three and my daughter was one. As a photographer, it's easy for me hide behind the camera. Clearly I'm going to be the best choice to capture memories of my family in a bomb way. Unfortunately, they might not have as many bomb captures of me. Selfies in the car with my seatbelt across my chest definitely don't count.

Kids grow fast though. They keep growing no matter how much you want them to stop. Time doesn't stop ticking by no matter the plans that you have for it. I have wasted so many irretrievable moments by not getting in the picture. I've opted out of capturing so many memories. I have wasted so much time in general during my kids' lives being worried about my weight. I've obsessed over being the fat mom. I don't go out as much as I should, I don't hang out as much as I should, and I absolutely don't enjoy as many physical activities with my children as I should. The fact of the matter is that my fear of putting myself on display for the judgment of the world has cost my children memories and experiences. They deserve better; so do I.

Having a daughter makes me aware of my responsibilities as her first role model. Whatever I would hope for her, whatever things that I would encourage her to do, however I would desire and expect her to value herself, I have to model for her first. Parents have tried and failed for a very long time at the "Do as I say and not as I do" style of parenting. It's often not even in the things that you teach verbally, but in your day-to-day lifestyle that what is normal is ingrained subconsciously. There are so many times nowadays when I look up and realize that I am doing something in a way that my mother did. It's all that I've been exposed to. Most times,

I don't have the wherewithal to even seek out a different way of doing things because I don't realize a different way even exists. So things like pampering myself, taking care of myself, showing up confidently, making demands of others, knowing my worth, and expressing my value will have to be intentionally modeled. I have to start with me if my daughter is going to learn not only what to do but why. Thankfully she's already highly confident, very strong willed, and outspoken. She's also a sensitive child, though. I need to be the one to shape the narrative of who she is, how she is, why she is, and what that means. And I'll shape it by the things that I say and I do as her role model. I am the first woman she will imitate. Even now, she literally wears my shoes and walks around the house. I listen to her talk to her dolls in my voice. I see in her so much of myself when I was her age, and for as different as we are, we have many, many similarities.

My daughter is currently thin and muscular. I doubt she'll endure the same insecurities I had and have with my weight. But she will indeed be insecure about something, because she's not perfect. And I plan to teach her that she's beautiful and worthy, even with those imperfections.

Renouncing the idolatry of weight loss will inevitably enable me to teach both of my children healthy ways to nurture and nourish themselves. I will not instill a habit of diet culture in either of them. I will not raise a son who objectifies women. I won't create a little boy who marries a woman and decides to look another way as soon as her weight fluctuates (and praise God that his father has been a role model in this regard). But I will teach them to value all people simply because God does (including themselves). I will teach them to eat foods in moderation. I will teach them the benefits of enjoying life, exercising, and trying new activities. They will know that exercise is not a punishment and it should not be regarded as something you do in response to some bad decision that you make. Instead, they'll learn that it's necessary maintenance for the beautiful temple we have been given to steward. I will teach them overall self-control. And I'll do this all through my words and actions.

That's why it's clearer to me than ever that changing my mindset now will inevitably help them both, both now and in the future. This experience is not just for my benefit but for their benefit, too. Because as I grow and go out into the world to gather wisdom, knowledge, and understanding those become their inheritance. As I heal, I stop them from being wounded early on by the tricks and schemes of the enemy. I can tell them what places to avoid, what thoughts to cast down, whom to embrace as allies, and how to distinguish enemies. For in as much as I am doing this for me, I'm doing this for them as well. That in and of itself is making this journey even more meaningful and important for me.

HUSTLE & GRINDING MY GEARS

I was 25 years old when Ray and I began our courtship and started seriously discussing marriage. One thing that I was absolutely sure about and that he needed to know and understand before making the decision to spend the rest of his life by my side: I would not be working for anyone by the age of 33.

I quit my full-time government career at the age of 32.

It wasn't a goal I'd set out to reach, but rather a part of a prophecy I had received when I was 22 or 23 years old while visiting a friend of a friend's father's church. It was my first and only prophetic word, and something within me believed and received it with a similar awe and excitement as the Virgin Mary.

Here's the thing though: I didn't know how or why, I only knew what. That what was that I would not be working for anyone by the age of 33.

In 2015, I walked away and never looked back. I had a vision. I had the prophetic word. I had a year-old business: Ali Watson Media, LLC. I had skills, gifts, and talent. I had a great personality. I made connections. I worked at my craft. I created dope projects. I had momentum.

I also had a problem. My confidence in God's ability to use me and my business ran out where my confidence in my appearance ended.

My weight became a heavy burden to my progress and success, not because I couldn't succeed while being overweight, but because I *believed* that I could not succeed because I was overweight. I could watch other "curvy" women rock out their brands with style, grace, and confidence but would resolve that that was for them and not me. I didn't have the personality to pull that off. I wasn't sassy, I wasn't saucy, I wasn't fun, I wasn't fly, I wasn't bold. I could describe myself in those ways when I weighed less, but now that I was bigger, I needed to lay low and not draw attention to myself.

In the age of social media, image is everything. Partly because we want our lives to look amazing, we share all of the awesome and none of the bad. It's gotten to a point that if you share the bad, people feel as though you need to seek therapy. I think that if all you show is good, then maybe you actually do need to seek therapy. There needs to be a balance. Any entrepreneur knows it's not always all good in the hood. There are many ups and downs. But the commonly held belief is that perception is reality. So a lot of us fake it until we make it. We show highlights and hint at troubles only once we've emerged victoriously. That's a slippery slope.

I share a lot of my struggles, not because I am negative, but because I love to spread hope and positivity. It's a part of my why and inherently a part of my makeup. To suppress it is uncomfortable and unnatural. Authenticity and transparency, especially in social media spaces, are supremely important to me. Conversely, though, when I win, I feel uncomfortable sharing those wins because I don't want people to feel bad about their losses or their pace in comparison, or to feel that I am arrogant. As a result, I think some people have pitied me or perceived my life as lacking in some way. It's not. My life is complete and full, and I am immensely happy. Except about how I look.

In the early years of growing my business, I learned from many marketing experts that in order to be successful, you have to show up where your people are and let them know what you have to offer and why they need it. Most of my people are on social media. So it's not really an option to go dark on social media for too long. And when you're active, you need to show your face, let them hear your voice, and share your day and personality. You need to offer value. You need to let them meet you because your vibe attracts your tribe. I understood all of that. I planned to do all of that. Eventually. Once I lost weight, I would be more comfortable to be visible and share my world. I put it on the backburner along with my other good intentions.

I still showed up on social media to post inspiration, engage, and show my work. Inevitably, that led to scrolling and consuming other people's content, too. It didn't take long to realize that social media can be a magnifier of your insecurities, no matter how meticulously you curate your feeds. It's so tough to know that you have potential and to see someone else living it out. At one time or another, we all fall into the comparison trap.

I know I did. I zeroed in on a particular person and obsessed over her. In reality, we could have been business besties. Instead, I grew increasingly annoyed with her. I would talk about her to everyone who would listen. I would get upset when she would post. She was confident. She was showing up. She was successful. She was winning. She was just like me in a lot of ways—except she had an itty-bitty waist, six-pack abs, and lady-like curves. Had I been more secure in who I was, I could have offered friendship and even mentorship in some areas. Instead, I saw her as competition.

We had similar businesses, our personal lives mirrored, we shared some of the same ambitions, we both loved God, and we were both driven and inspiring, but the enemy convinced me that the biggest difference between us—and what put her ahead of me—was that she looked the part and I didn't. She had the skills, the drive, the talent, *and the looks*. She had the total package. She was what I *could be* but wasn't. She could show up and I couldn't. And *that's* why she was more successful than I was. It was unfair. I was jealous.

I made the same mistake for both of us: I attributed success and failure primarily to our physical appearance. The truth of the matter is that we are both blessed and called by God for His purposes. We are both growing and learning. Whether she gains a ton of weight or I lose a ton of weight, any and all success we enjoy before and after that point will be by God's hand and for His glory. What really matters for the success of our businesses and our lives overall is our faith.

Nevertheless, my jealousy would make me feel as though she was arrogant and attention-seeking. I grew sick and tired of seeing her posting pictures of herself, her successes, her clients, and her husband. Basically anything and everything she did was an excuse for me to scoff and roll my eyes. As a way to affirm and exalt myself, I would take pride in my humility. I would try to boost myself with assertions that people were visiting my sites and working with my company because of the work only and not because of me. Deep down inside, I knew that that wasn't true. I felt the conviction of God telling me to show up, speak up, use my voice, encourage others, share my story, and share His Gospel. I refused to do so because I didn't want to be judged. I judge myself harshly enough, and in reality, I could not deal with the thought of others rejecting me on the basis of my biggest insecurity: how fat I had gotten.

Of course, my business suffered. The marketing experts are experts for a reason. It has always been profitable, but it could be so much more. It could be more impactful, more in demand, and more in line with the vision I saw for it when I set out on the journey to pursue it. However, my faith was in my weight loss, in my performance, and in myself and not in God. I hoped that one day I would lose the weight so that I could be the total package—so that I could show up, put myself out there, and be perfect enough for my haters to be silent and for my supporters to be proud. I believed I was being honest with myself and humble about my position until God showed me that I didn't know what humility meant.

"Humility wants the light to shine before man so that God can be glorified. Insecurity hides from the light. Arrogance longs for the light." —Keith Battle

I was tasked with studying humility, not because I wasn't being humble but because what I was really doing was shrinking. The best way to be humble is to be authentic and truly you, to take risks and to shine and stumble while giving God the glory. Humble yourself before the Lord, and there is no way not to be humble before men. He can lift you up in the eyes of men. There are no doors that he can't open that your posturing would have. You have to be careful when building a brand that you build it in the right image.

"Humble yourself before the Lord and He will lift you up."
—James 4:10 (NLT)

There was a really funny commercial from Sprite in the late 90s with three really street Black basketball players who turned out to be actors who studied Shakespeare. That commercial has always tickled me. But it's also stuck with me, especially when building my own brand. Image is nothing. Thirst is everything. When you are creating an image, you crave attention, and that's true whether you're in a confident position to seek it out or sitting on the sidelines wishing you could. Creating an image is pointless. We want people to accept us, so we create an acceptable image. The image is not us, though, so in fact, people are not accepting us but the image. The moment you deviate from that image, people will get confused about who you are, and ultimately, they will reject you.

Instead, we should thirst for God. It's like when you're eating all day long, but in reality, you need to drink some water. We're so dehydrated. We need the Living Water, but we're snacking on likes and follows, awards and accolades, being fully booked with full bank accounts and never truly being satisfied. What we truly desire is an unconditional love and acceptance that can never be taken from us. From that space, we can truly understand who we are and show up authentically and without fear of rejection because we know whose we are. We have unlimited access the source that fills and satisfies us.

Through my studies and actions, I've seen the results of humbling myself before Him, showing up physically, in spite of my flaws. He, in turn, sent the attention I was seeking. I didn't need to change one thing. I didn't *have to* wear a mask of a different personality, put on a full face of makeup before I hit Instagram, or lose 80 pounds before pressing record. Image is nothing. It's a façade. It fades, and it can't be maintained. Thirsting for God is real, and the Living Water never dries up. It never requires us to adjust anything about ourselves to partake in it.

I had to learn to trust God and allow Him to lead me in my work. I had to allow Him to show me how He made me specifically and resolve to shine in my unique makeup. Simply *be* who you are and obey the thirst in your heart: your why, your passions, your giftings, and your talents. Excel in those things, share those gifts with the world, and you won't be able to be denied. Don't deny His direction when what others are doing seems to be the way to do it. That's their path, not yours. You may not have what you need for someone else's journey, but you have exactly what you need for your own.

A couple of months ago, I felt led to reach out to the woman I mentioned earlier in this section. I sent her a message and confessed and apologized for how I had been badmouthing and jealous of her. She had no idea but responded with grace and love. We made peace. She shared that I was the seventh woman to express feeling that way, and I told her that there was a reason God had allowed these things to be revealed to her. I encouraged her to continue on with her sharing, her winning, her hard work, her confidence, and her sharing her faith. In spite of what we or anyone else felt, our feelings had nothing to do with her and everything to do with what God was working out in us. I reminded her to continue to allow Him to use her because she is an inspiration to many. A few weeks later, she suffered a physical ailment that affected her appearance in a major way. She shared her journey to recovery. She didn't hide or wait until she got better. She continued to show up. She continued to work. She continued to win, and it had nothing to do with how beautiful she is or how she felt about her looks. Her faith healed her, and by sharing the process, she inspired countless others to have more faith in God. Moreover, it disproved what I believed about needing the total package to succeed. That woman is a force. So am I. And with God, we are unstoppable.

If He tells you how you are supposed to do it, do it that way. Believe Him. Be humble. Go forth and be great, just the way He made you.

"Therefore, since we are surrounded by such a huge crowd of witnesses to the life of faith, let us strip off every weight that slows us down, especially the sin that so easily trips us up. And let us run with endurance the race God has set before us." — *Hebrews 12:1 (NLT)*

PART II

Okay, It's Time to Check the Map

Getting over Our Weight and into Our Purpose

Now that I know better, I have to do better, and ultimately, I'll be better. But this part of the book is less about me and more about us. This is the part where we do the work: the heavy mental lifting that comes with making a mindset change that will lead to a lifestyle change. My prayer is that through the Word and these insights and advice, that you and I not only do things differently, but most of all experience the *freedom* that comes with embracing the view and perspective of the world that God has shared with us. I also pray that once we possess it, this freedom, we will fight mightily to hold on to it (no matter what culture says or other people believe).

Every victory I have had has started with a surrender. When I got married, I surrendered my self-centeredness. When I had children, I surrendered my body, my ability to move about freely, and my finances. When God urged me to leave my "good gubment" job, I surrendered my sense of stability and security. When I started therapy, I surrendered my sense of privacy and even parts of my ego. When I gave my life to Christ, I surrendered my prerogative to sin freely, unencumbered by the conviction of the Holy Spirit. These are all experiences I wouldn't trade now. These are all experiences that I know that God desired for me. But getting my desires to align with His desires required me to surrender my will. This book is another surrender. It's a heart decision, coupled with a public declaration, and even a rallying call to my sisters (His daughters) to surrender and align our thoughts, plans, and reasons for our weight loss with His. I'm confident that by doing so, we'll gain victory in that area, too.

What happens when two factions on the same team are fighting for the same cause but trying to get there in different ways? A civil war wages from within. Only one can be in charge here. You can only go in one direction at a time according to one plan at a time. God gave us free will. He's not going to force you to do it His way. But if you *are* going to do it His way, you must surrender your own. Once you do, you may find that it's actually more efficient and less frustrating.

I remember when my daughter was a toddler. There were many times where she tried to tell me that she "could do it" herself. Sometimes I would allow her to do things that I'd been doing for ten times the amount of time she'd been alive. I'd be standing there with all of my wisdom, knowledge, experience, and hand-eye coordination while she would try to zip her jacket up. I'd watch her grow frustrated, tears welling up in her eyes, hands becoming more frantic, patience growing shorter. I wanted to help but would keep my distance, because every time I went to step in, she would exclaim something about how she could do it.

Clearly, she couldn't do it.

Yes, I gave her the freedom to try, but she didn't really have the ability to accomplish the task on her own. Sometimes, I realize that that is how God is standing there looking at me. With all of the wisdom, knowledge, experience, and solutions in His hands, I swat him away while I'm screaming, "No, God! I can do it!" Meanwhile, He simply watches me as I grow frustrated with my fumbling hands and short patience. What's crazy is that at some point I will even have the nerve to yell out, "God, why aren't you helping me?" Because I told Him not to. Duh. It sucks having to learn things the hard way; so much wasted energy, so much wasted time.

What transforms a surrender into a victory? Not what: who. We're told in Romans 8:28, "And we know that in all things God works for the good of those who love him, who have been called according to his purpose" (NIV). Whatever you've decided to surrender to God, just know that He can do exceedingly abundantly above all that you can hope for that thing, than you can dream for it, wish for it, imagine for it, and especially do *with it* on your own. If you keep laying that thing down on the altar, He will keep giving you a ram in the bush. He will stay with you. He will work for you. This applies to your body, too. We are to present our bodies as a living sacrifice.

"Therefore, I urge you, brothers and sisters, in view of God's mercy, to offer your bodies as a living sacrifice, holy and pleasing to God-this is true worship." —Romans 12:1 (TNIV)

What is a sacrifice? Well, since we no longer slaughter animals as a sacrifice, at this point, it's simply an offering, a gift. Have you ever given a gift? When you give a gift, you don't try to control how the person uses it or what they do with it. You offer it to them for them to do as they please because you want them to have it. The word sacrifice in this day and age has such a negative connotation. It denotes a feeling of loss, a feeling of struggle, as if it's going to hurt. Sometimes, yes, sacrifices do hurt, and sometimes they cause a deficit. But ultimately, the sacrifice is less about how it will hurt or disadvantage you and more about the heart behind it. Why are you okay with the hurt or deficit? Is it a ritual? It is for show? Or is it because you have a relationship with the recipient? And even if it hurts you, you want them to enjoy the gift, right? You want her face to light up when she receives the gift, right? You may even want to repay the joy you got when you received a gift from her. As believers, God's mercy is our greatest gift. Surrendering and laying our will on the altar is perhaps our greatest gift to Him in return—our truest form of worship as we learned in the scripture above, Just like the widow's offering in Luke 21:1-4 (NLT), "While Jesus was in the Temple, he watched the rich people dropping their gifts in the collection box. Then a poor widow came by and dropped in two small coins. 'I tell you the truth,' Jesus said, "this poor widow has given more than all the rest of them. For they have given a tiny part of their surplus, but she, poor as she is, has given everything she has.'"

You may go to church and tithe your 10 percent, give freely to the less fortunate, rescue friends and family in dire straits, volunteer your time, so on and so forth, but like the rich in scripture, that may not actually affect your heart. Those aren't the things that we are struggling to keep close. We can give to others. But can we give up our ideas about our weight? Or ideas about the abundance of sexiness that we're "entitled" to? Can we give up the idea that one day we will have it all if we can just get this one area together? The idea of perfection? Mindset is sacrificable. Control is sacrificable. Let's lay them down. He has something better for us. We have to believe that.

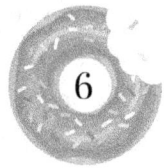

6

So, What's Your Purpose?

In order for this book and the subtitle to make sense, we have to agree on this: your purpose comes from God. And also: you are not made aware of what it is until after your salvation. Prior to your salvation, your purpose, actions, and direction are self serving, self pleasing, and for your own benefit. Once you're saved, your focus moves from yourself and onto the Lord. This is usually when you start to seek to be used by God and to understand your true purpose.

This is a purpose that you pursue deliberately. It is true that God is the great conductor. He moves all things together at once, creating life as we know it. So with that in mind, it's very possible that you have been moving toward God's purpose for your life without even knowing it and without submitting completely to him. A great example is the Pharaoh of Egypt in Exodus. Though his actions and pride did not appear to have anything to do with God, the Lord still had a strong hand in how that whole situation played out. He orchestrated from start to finish how His people would be delivered out of Egypt.

I believe that there are two steps to uncovering your purpose in life. The first: call and ask God. The second: listen. Pretty simple, right? Not necessarily. I forgot to mention the prerequisites. You have to first get to know God, build a relationship with Him, submit to Him, and trust Him.

There are a lot of people who know of God without realizing the need to get to know Him personally. There is a difference between having religion and having a relationship with God. Religion involves a set of rules and traditions. It lacks compassion and is behavior centric. People use it to show others how good they are. They use it to pridefully place themselves above others. One could be self-righteous and successful at religion because of what one does or does not do. But that does not leave much room for grace or mercy from God. Religion also excludes a lot of people because they can't live up to its standard of perfection. Religion is usually why people don't like religion. Two things are true: people are flawed and people will fail. So when people who love religion purport perfection and come up short, they look like hypocrites. Untrustworthy hypocrites and people on the outside looking in throw out the baby, the bath water, the bath tub and the bath tub manufacturer. They want no parts of it. I can't say that I blame them.

On the other hand, if you know and have a relationship with God, then you know that you absolutely pale in comparison to Him. There is zero room to boast in His presence—and we're always in His presence. He *is* perfection.

And even though we are flawed and sinful, He still wants to kick it with us, which is why He saved us by grace through faith. It was a gift; one that can't be explained away or paid back by religious actions. His love is unconditional. He doesn't require perfection from you, but profession. Romans 10:9 (NLT) assures us that "If you declare with your mouth, 'Jesus is Lord,' and believe in your heart that God raised him from the dead, you will be saved." It's a freely given gift that we can choose to accept.

Once you accept that gift, you go on a journey to get to know God. That includes reading your Bible, praying often, joining a church fellowship, and taking up your cross daily and following Him. Through having a relationship with God, you learn His personality. It's very similar to having a relationship with your mother in that you know what she expects, how she reacts, her rules, her idiosyncrasies, and many other things about her because you have spent a lot of time with her. Just in my experience with God, I've learned that He is just, compassionate, holy, generous, sovereign, powerful, and majestic yet accessible because He wants to be. He loves us. I know that He's awesome and worthy of my reverence and praise. I know that He's my father, my leader, my healer, my friend, and my guidance counselor. I know that He is wise beyond all understanding. I've learned all these things just by intentionally spending time with Him and getting to know Him. And just by getting to know Him, I know that there's so much about Him I have yet to discover. That's actually really exciting.

Once you know God like this, you understand how much more sense it makes to submit to him, not just out of fear, but out of love and reverence, too. In doing so, you acknowledge that His plan is better, His will is perfect, and His ways are greater than your own. It's not easy to do. No one gets it right all of the time. My life verse is Proverbs 3:5-6 (NLT):

> "Trust in the Lord with all your heart;
> do not depend on your own understanding.
> Seek his will in all you do,
> and he will show you which path to take."

I'm so guilty of trusting without leaning. I fancy myself a pretty smart cookie. I've accomplished a lot in my lifetime. I'm pretty creative. I'm responsible. A leader. But none of that compares with the titles the Lord holds nor the things He's accomplished in and outside of time. I have a tendency to trust that He's given me a task but not seek His advice on how and when to carry it out. But part of trusting Him includes leaning on His understanding of things. It includes acknowledging Him with every step you take. I know people who take this quite literally. Someone I know wakes up every day and asks God what to wear in the morning. I don't do it daily, but I've done it before. In my instance, finding the right outfit was becoming stressful, so I prayed and asked God to lead me to something. I pulled together a super cute outfit right from my closet and had a great evening. It is wise to trust God because He is wise. It takes the pressure off you to be right and frees you up to simply be used. Practicing seeking Him in such small things will aid in being sensitive enough to learn, accept, and fulfill your God-given life's purpose.

Most likely, your purpose is going to be formed around your talents and your abilities. Every person is different but each possesses God-given gifts, spiritual or otherwise. Your talents may be used on a large scale, or their reach may seem small. But how significant the world believes your gifts and talents to be does not matter. What is important, what brings value to them, is using those gifts and talents in accordance with God's will and purpose.

That's to say that if God has given you a specific gift or talent, own it! Don't covet someone else's because it seems more glamorous, more fun, or maybe even easier. Take the gifts and talents that He has given to you and fulfill the purpose for which you were created. Be obedient. Just because you *can* do something does not mean that you *should*. And this is why it's important to know and have a relationship with God: fear, doubt, naysayers, and experience will tempt you to do the thing that makes more sense but is miles away from the path to your purpose. This is the reason Jesus told well-meaning, ride-or-die Peter to "Get behind me Satan!" when He tried to tell Jesus that Jesus's death wouldn't go down the way that Jesus shared. Jesus *knew* what God said and that trumped what anyone else said. Even when He prayed for God to change his mind about His fate, He corrected

Himself in the same breath, saying, "Nevertheless, not my will, but your will be done." Jesus laid down his will, and we all have the victory because of it. Believe it or not, the whole body of Christ benefits from your obedience, too.

I was listening to one of my favorite radio stations one day and heard a commercial for a weight loss product. On it, a woman was excitedly giving a testimonial. She was so pleased with the results and so confident in them that she called the company up and asked to be a representative to distribute the product for them! How awesome would it be if we were *that* pleased with the Lord and His grace, mercy, and goodness? If we enthusiastically sought Him out to ask if we could represent Him based on how He had changed our lives? It would be wonderful. In fact, that is how it should be. And essentially, that's what we're doing when we operate in our God-given purpose in order to bring Him the glory, honor and praise. God is working in you, giving you His desires, and empowering you to do what is pleasing to Him. So grow in your gifts and talents.

Proverbs 22:29 (NLT) says, "Do you see any truly competent workers? They will serve kings rather than working for ordinary people."

Gifts and talents are naturally poured into you by God at your conception. However, you have to take the time to develop these into skills. The promise of Proverbs 22:29 is that once you develop those talents and go above and beyond to become skilled, you will become elite. The truth of the matter is that we, as children of God, are not average.

Therefore, we should be constantly striving to stay above average. The confidence you gain from investing your time, energy, and sometimes resources into developing your talents into skills will assist you in overcoming obstacles to moving into your purpose. Trust me, it won't be in vain. Study, practice, and become an expert in order to distinguish yourself, and as the proverb says, you'll stand before kings. Strive to be excellent and you'll be rewarded for the hard work you put into it. Proverbs 14:23 (NLT) says, "Work brings profit, but mere talk leads to poverty!"

Beyond the physical and financial abundance are mental and spiritual abundance as well. These are the promises that you receive with Matthew 6:33 (the scriptural basis for this book). Think of the pro athlete who's going after the championship trophy. He might receive fame, sponsorships, endorsements, the cover of the box of Wheaties, and more, but those are all added on as a result of setting the goal, putting in the work, and staying the course to be the best. Those things were never his goal to begin with. The trappings of seeking God's Kingdom and His righteousness fall into the category of "the things we need." For so long, one of the things I "needed" was to lose weight. I felt that once I had hit the right number on the scale, then I could effectively pursue God, His righteousness, and His will and purpose for my life. You feel this way too, don't you? We're so wrong, though. We don't need to seek after *any* of the things we *think* we need. We only need to seek Him.

"I knew you before I formed you in your mother's womb. Before you were born I set you apart and appointed you as my prophet to the nations." —Jeremiah 1:5 (NLT)

According to Jeremiah 1:5, God created an elaborate holy plan for your life before your life was even a thing. Most likely, the events that have occurred in your life have been shaping you for and pushing you toward your purpose, your weight concerns included. Once you come to know Him only a fraction of the extent to which He knows you, once you open up your heart to Him and submit your own will, you will be in the best position possible to shake your fears and step into your purpose, because you'll know nothing is impossible for God, even using an overweight woman as a brand ambassador for His divine purpose. Trust God. He's put everything within you to do everything He's purposed for you to do.

So, what is your purpose?

No, Seriously, He's Sending You— Yes, You!

It is so easy to lose sight of who God is in our lives. There is an old adage that goes, "Seeing is believing." We humans have a tendency to depend on our intellect and experiences when it comes to understanding and overcoming the hardships that we endure. By doing so, we alienate God. Not one to impose, He will often leave us to our own devices. When those fail (as they inevitably will), He returns and does what was impossible for us to do: fixes it.

A great example is found in the Book of Judges, Chapter Six. When the Israelites were wilding out and had (once again) done evil in the eyes of the Lord, He allowed them several years of poverty and great suffering. This time, the Israelites' evil deed was putting their trust in the gods of the people on whose land they were living. They were worshipping and praising them, but soon enough, they realized these gods were unable to deliver them from the hands of their oppressive enemies, the Midianites. So they returned to God, the God of their ancestors, with pleas for help. When He responded, He not only reminded them of why they were in the situation they were in, He proved to them that it was He, only, who could and would rescue them from it. And He did.

When the Israelites turned their hearts and faith back toward God, He was pleased to turn his favor back on them. Here's how all of this applies to you and me: the Lord is not concerned with perfection but with integrity and character. God often used imperfect people to perform the missions most integral in building the body of believers.

Enter Gideon.

He described himself as the least of his family, a family that was pretty whack in the first place, being a part of the weakest clan in Manasseh (Verse 15). He said all of this of himself even after the angel of God had confirmed him and his gift, calling him "mighty warrior" (Verse 12). The angel even confirmed God's presence was with Gideon. And yet Gideon still had doubts. Does that sound familiar to you? Has God given you an assignment and affirmed you and even given you the ability to carry it out, and yet you still can't believe? Has he called you a name that you can't fathom being associated with—oh, gifted speaker, innovative entrepreneur, or fitness coach? Have you heard His voice yet still can't wrap your mind around the fact that He is present with you and wants to guide you to success?

Well, faith is believing and *then* seeing. Trust God, believe God, and allow Him to show you what He knew from the beginning concerning you and your talents. Gideon did. It wasn't an easy journey to victory, but I believe Gideon's story demonstrates God's patience with us, especially when we are sincerely seeking His will, even if with a bit of apprehension. In Jeremiah 29:11 (NLT), God says, "For I know the plans that I have for you, plans to give you hope and a future." I believe God is excited about the excellent job He has done in creating our individual life plans and is willing to put forth the extra effort of building our faith so that we can fulfill the purpose for which He created us.

At the beginning of Gideon's story, we find that he had zero confidence that God was present with him and his people. Because of the severity and hopelessness of his circumstances, he lacked the vision to see it improve. On top of that, he had low self-esteem. He thought little of himself because of his position in society. But what stands out most about Gideon is that even though he doubted, when prompted, he still took action to allow God to prove who God was. Not only that, but through his trust and interactions with God, Gideon allowed the Lord to redefine his own identity. Through action and obedience, he was able to build his confidence in the Lord and in himself. Looking at his experiences, we are able to learn how and take away some useful tools in developing our own faith and understanding our own identity.

Gideon was given the assignment to save Israel from the hand of the Midianites. This assignment was a big deal. His fear told him that he was definitely not the man for the job. God said otherwise. Gideon had learned from his relatives that historically God was true to His word, but he had yet to experience it for himself. Even still, Gideon was not happy with the status quo, so he opened his heart enough to hear God out. It couldn't get any worse, right?

The first (and most valuable) lesson I learned from Gideon's story is that if you're going to move with God and live out His purpose for your life, you have to get rid of any other god you've placed before Him. Consequently, you might upset other people. And that's exactly what happened. God commanded Gideon to tear down the altar his father had for Baal and the Asherah pole that stood beside it. In its place, Gideon was to build an altar to God and sacrifice his father's second bull using the wood from the Asherah pole to fuel the fire.

"So Gideon took ten of his servants and did as the Lord had commanded. But he did it at night because he was afraid of the other members of his father's household and the people of the town."
—Judges 6:27 (NLT)

And rightfully so. The people were big mad. They wanted to kill him. Thankfully his father was a quick thinker and a smooth talker. He persuaded the crowd to let Baal deal with Gideon if Baal was indeed a god.

You might have to tear down some altars that others have erected, whether physical or ideological, before you can get into your God-given purpose. For me it's ideological. I have to tear down the thought that losing weight is going to fix or change everything, even my relationship with and usefulness to God. It's not a popular notion. I have no doubt that people judge me or pity me when I talk about it. Some might even oppose me because they've built a brand around diet culture, obsessive exercise, and Transformation Tuesday. Sharing such a perspective can affect their bottom line if enough of the people they are targeting listen to and embrace it. Maybe what God is calling you to dethrone will make people reject you, too. It might make people angry with you. Worst of all, it might make people want to kill you. But do it anyway. If God is for you, who can be against you?

Let your experience with God override your experience with this world. There are so many factors that inhibit believers from stepping into the purpose that God has set before them. One of the most influential is that most of us are inherently people pleasers. Something that the Lord has called you to do might not sit particularly well with another person. Your friends may not agree with your decision to end your relationship. Your parents may think that you've wasted their money because you changed your major instead of going forward toward law school like you promised. Your boyfriend might be confused with your decision to move out but not end the relationship. Because these people have a strong influence in your life and may have helped you along your journey, you hold their opinions in high regard. Even if you have not already revealed your plans to them, you've anticipated that they would think or feel negatively about your assignment. Even the thought keeps you stagnant. It's not wrong for them to care about you or to give you advice, but it is wrong for you to disobey God out of fear of them and their opinions. It is wiser to move in silence and obey God (like how Gideon moved in the dark of night) than to openly please people and miss the move of God. Ultimately, Gideon's act of obedience led to him saving the very people who were up at dawn demanding his head. Who knows how your obedience and the fulfillment of your purpose will bless your loved ones down the line? God knows. Trust Him.

The second lesson I learned from Gideon's story is that it's okay to ask God for a sign. If you are unsure about the direction that God is really telling you to go, just ask. I am sure He appreciates the fact that you are focused on staying within His will.

"Then Gideon said to God, 'If you are truly going to use me to rescue Israel as you promised, prove it to me in this way. I will put a wool fleece on the threshing floor tonight. If the fleece is wet with dew in the morning but the ground is dry, then I will know that you are going to help me rescue Israel as you promised.' And that is just what happened. When Gideon got up early the next morning, he squeezed the fleece and wrung out a whole bowlful of water.

Then Gideon said to God, 'Please don't be angry with me, but let me make one more request. Let me use the fleece for one more test. This time let the fleece remain dry while the ground around it is wet with dew.' So that night God did as Gideon asked. The fleece was dry in the morning, but the ground was covered with dew." —Judges 6:36-39 (NLT)

Secret Donuts

Man, I rarely get a direct, physical response from God like this. That would be amazing. Nevertheless, God confirms his assignments for me through consistent messaging that pops up so many times in so many different ways that it can't be a coincidence. Recently, I felt the urge to send some money to a friend who I know is struggling financially. I woke up to the scripture of the day being about giving, then when I listened to my favorite podcast on the way to drop my kids off at school, it was about giving, too. The friend then called me out of the blue to just check on me. For me, those are all signs that God is the one telling me to do the things he places on my heart to do. Gideon's signs didn't make sense scientifically, but that's how he knew it was truly God. Only God could defy nature. And I experience the same thing: when something doesn't make sense but feels right, I know that it's God moving. Like when He tells me to give during times when I should be the one receiving; if I do, somehow my lack becomes more than enough.

God used and uses signs to reassure us that He is with us and that He is truly sending us. He knows our hearts, He knows our fears, and He knows our apprehension, so He's patient with us, just as He was with Gideon. Trust is a huge part of any healthy relationship, so it makes sense that we are able to ask questions and seek further understanding, just like Gideon. God won't show us the whole plan though; he will illuminate the step we're on so that we have faith enough to simply take the next one. That's what He did with Gideon. God responded positively to Gideon's request for a sign, but there was no way that Gideon could have predicted what God would do next.

"So Jerub-baal (that is, Gideon) and his army got up early and went as far as the spring of Harod. The armies of Midian were camped north of them in the valley near the hill of Moreh. The Lord said to Gideon, 'You have too many warriors with you. If I let all of you fight the Midianites, the Israelites will boast to me that they saved themselves by their own strength. Therefore, tell the people, "Whoever is timid or afraid may leave this mountain and go home."' So 22,000 of them went home, leaving only 10,000 who were willing to fight.

But the Lord told Gideon, 'There are still too many! Bring them down to the spring, and I will test them to determine who will go with you and who will not.' When Gideon took his warriors down to the water, the Lord told him, 'Divide the men into two groups. In one group put all those who cup water in their hands and lap it up with their tongues like dogs. In the other group put all those who kneel down and drink with their mouths in the stream.' Only 300 of the men drank from their hands. All the others got down on their knees and drank with their mouths in the stream.

The Lord told Gideon, 'With these 300 men I will rescue you and give you victory over the Midianites. Send all the others home.' So Gideon collected the provisions and rams' horns of the other warriors and sent them home. But he kept the 300 men with him." —Judges 7:1-8 (NLT)

Secret Donuts

With which would you rather fight a war: 22,000 men or 300? I bet Gideon felt the same way. But God wanted the glory. After all, it was God whom the Israelites asked to rescue them from the hands of the Midianites. Gideon was merely the vessel that God would use to answer their prayers. On the journey to reaching your purpose you may experience obstacles, losses, and handicaps. Some people you thought would support you will go missing. Some might outright oppose you. Resources you've wisely stockpiled will be consumed by circumstances beyond your control. Monkey wrenches will fly at your plans. You'll doubt that you heard what you heard—that the assignment was really from God at all. But slow your roll. Consider that perhaps God is allowing these things to happen so that He will get the glory and not you or anyone else. It's very possible that what He will do with and through you will look like a miracle. It won't make sense to people. And for that reason they will believe in Him, glorify Him, and turn their hearts to Him. That's the ultimate goal.

Another thing to note is that Gideon was in constant communication with God. God spoke, he listened. He spoke, God listened. Faith comes by hearing and hearing by the word of God. From the beginning, Gideon had an idea of how this mission was supposed to go, but at every turn, God revealed His strategy, and it looked totally different. Gideon may not have understood how 300 men could stand against Midian and their allies. But the cool thing is that they didn't even have to. The other army ended up turning on and killing themselves before Gideon and his men even had to lift a finger. God will not always solve your problems the way you imagine He will. Your imagination is limited. Your perception of "possible" is limited to what you have learned or experienced. God *is* experience; He cannot be limited by your imagination. Nothing is impossible with God.

God doesn't need anything from you but your obedience. He doesn't need you to look the part; He only needs you to be willing to play it. You may think little of yourself, but even carrying extra weight can be the vehicle God uses to drive people to freedom and a heart change. It doesn't depend on you doing anything that He doesn't ask you to do.

I emphasize this because you need to understand that you can't qualify yourself. God qualifies the called. It has taken me a while to embrace this. I've felt close to God. I've been excited about the vision He's given me. Yet I didn't feel good enough to perform my mission. I couldn't accept God's acceptance because I couldn't accept myself. There was a time when I looked up scriptures to condemn myself. I was so spiritual that I didn't want to be perceived as vain or as if I was too concerned with being beautiful (even though I was). Instead, I pointed to scripture as an acceptable reason for obsessing over losing weight, because if I did it for God then it would more commendable. I misused the Word to confirm my bad opinion of myself. I wanted spiritual proof that I was in sin and needed a new angle to push myself to lose weight.

I would look up verses like Philippians 3:18-19(NLT): "For, as I have often told you before and now tell you again even with tears, many live as enemies of the cross of Christ.

Their destiny is destruction, their god is their stomach, and their glory is in their shame. Their mind is set on earthly things" (emphasis my own).

I would use scripture all out of context, akin to when they used the Bible to justify slavery. I would cite disappointment in myself for saying that I loved God but didn't show that love by honoring my temple and losing weight. I had to do better if I was a Christian. And in a sense, that was true, because, as we will discuss later, you only get one body to live out your purpose, so you should honor and take care of it. But the foundation of that care and honor has to be right. As I mentioned, I would use these scriptures to condemn myself, but the root of that condemnation was cultural and not scriptural. So then the scriptures became added fuel to the flames of my body shame and body image issues. I would totally skip over the parts of the word like Psalms 139 and John 3:16 that speak of God's love for me, unwisely denying the unconditional love that he supplied whether I was a size 6 or a size 26.

Let's park there for a minute. Is it possible that you believe that *even* God loves you less because you're overweight? Really think about it. Say it out loud if you must. Call that lie all the way out. Do you believe He is more disappointed in you than of women who are thinner and more confident? Do you believe He's waiting on you to make changes to your size before He will give you a platform, the spotlight, or the green light to do what He's called you to do? This is a friendly reminder that that is not faith, that's performance based. He's not asking you to perform. The person who does the thing gets the credit, and we already established that God wants the glory, right? Again, there is *nothing* that you have to do of your own volition to get qualified. You only need to be obedient to God. And that starts with having a relationship with Him, trusting Him, and believing Him. Believe Him when He says that He loves you and when He says that He made you just as He wanted you to be. Believe that He has a plan for you (and even though it looks different sometimes, it really *is* to give you a hope and a future). Your purpose is more important than your pride. You've got to stop protecting your ego and move past your fear of judgment. Allow God to put you out there so that He can also show you how He can and will protect you. I like to think of it this way: if God's will is a puzzle, we each have a piece. That piece is your purpose. Your piece might contain a part of the vast blue sky and be seemingly insignificant. It might contain one of two distinct elements so that it stands out and can be easily placed. Either way, your piece is uniquely shaped and one of a kind. In order to see the completed big picture God is trying to show us all, you need to be a team player and add your piece. Your piece connects other pieces. There is no one like you, and no one can do what you do. You are fearfully and wonderfully made. I believe everyone has a purpose. It doesn't even have be epic or grand. You could be a Dr. Martin Luther King, Jr. or you could be the person responsible for raising a Dr. Martin Luther King, Jr. Both are important. Whether you are here to influence millions or only one, make it your mission to do just that. Trust Him when He says "Go now in the strength you have…" just like He said to Gideon. You have enough. You are enough. Right now.

Go.

If God Is for You...

Have you ever been booed before? I have. I've stood at a podium prepared to give a speech in front of hundreds of people while they booed me.

Picture it. Michigan. 1999.

A high school junior sits on a stage before an auditorium packed with everyone in the entire school. Students. Faculty. Everyone.

She's the class president, has been for the last two years, and on this day, each class president has to give a speech on the state of the class. No big deal. She's done it twice before.

Today, however, is different. A few guys near the front, with most of whom she's friends, have a new thing. In their deepest voices, they chant a throaty "Heyyyyy." It's cute. It's funny. She's even chanted with them at times.

As the principal announces her name, she stands to approach the podium. The guys start their chant. She smiles at their predictability. Then something unpredictable happens: the crowd starts to boo. Almost immediately, though, up rises a chorus of "yays." Then back and forth, like waves of an indecisive sea, the "yays" and "boos" continue.

Clearly, the baritone of the boys' voices has been mistaken for disapproval. She stands there, speechless, eyebrows raised, eyes swinging from one side of the crowded room of over 1000 people to the other. Her heart is beating rapidly; but oddly, everything else is moving in slow motion. Slow, like the moment you meet the love of your life or the moment you find yourself in danger—your senses are heightened to catch every little detail, every color, shape, and action, because in this moment you innately know that this moment will be a defining one.

And it was.

Back in real time, the teachers are up silencing the students and restoring order. And then the room is eerily silent. Everyone is waiting.

So what does she do? Does she grab her belongings and run out of the auditorium sobbing uncontrollably? Does she release her Southeast side with a slew of obscenities because she's "bout it, it bout it"? (Remember, it's 1999.)

No. She smiles and says, "Okay" and does what she came to do: read the speech she prepared on the State of the Class of 2001. When she finishes, she smiles again, thanks them, and returns to her seat.

Then the senior class president gets up and goes smooth off on what he referred to as an immature and ungrateful student body for disrespecting a leader they elected. She doesn't exactly disapprove of that response either.

Secret Donuts

The important thing to note is that I went ahead and gave my speech. Things happened that I didn't expect and over which I had no control, but still I went forward with what I came to do. It was a great life lesson for me. Up until that point, I was aware of the possibility of people not liking me, but never was it so blatantly obvious that there were *actually* people in this world who, probably for no real, tangible, justifiable, valid reason, did not like me. And they were just waiting for an "acceptable" moment to demonstrate it. And demonstrate it they did. In that moment, however, I could not allow it to distract me from my purpose. That incident occurred almost 20 years ago, and even still there are people who don't like me. And just like then, that fact will not, should not, and cannot stop me from living out my purpose. The same is true of you.

I've heard it said that "If you live for people's acceptance, you'll die from their rejection." It's so important to stay neutral to people's opinions. People don't have to co-sign your purpose or your dreams. I'm not saying to isolate yourself; wise counsel, community, and mentorship is very important on your journey. But these people should be like the supporters standing on the side of the road with a cup of water while you run the marathon. The route is mapped out by God; they are just there to give you tips, refreshment, resources, and encouragement (not to tell you which way to go).

One concept that's key to helping me keep everything in perspective is reminding myself that all I do as an artist is for an audience of One (that "One" being God). I was first introduced to it while reading *The Heart of the Artist* by Rory Noland. It's a book with great perspective, and I read it every time I take on a new artistic endeavor. In order to avoid distraction, I try to give God my attention early on. This book reminds me to seek his guidance, helps me adjust my attitude, and warns of the pitfalls of having the wrong focus. I apply this to more than my art. I apply it to my entire life.

Not everyone will like you. If everyone likes you, then you're doing something wrong. At the very least you're living a very inauthentic life. If everyone likes you and you like everybody, pause and reflect. If everything that you say and do is acceptable to everyone, then somebody is lying (and most likely, that somebody is you). The most interesting and well-loved people—celebrities, religious leaders, intellectuals, the president, heck, even the Messiah—are polarizing. They usually believe something so incredibly deeply and with so much conviction that it forces people to one side or the other about them and their beliefs. And that's okay! Being explicit and real actually has its benefits. From a space of authenticity is where one can have the most influence.

A few years ago, not long after I started building my business, I felt an urge to attend a one-day branding intensive with a branding expert I followed on social media. It was in Atlanta, Georgia; I live near Washington, DC. Yet within a matter of two hours of the expert's announcement, I had pulled all the strings to book my flight, pay for the intensive (which was nearly 1000 dollars), clear it with my husband so that he could take my son to school on his very first day of kindergarten, and arrange childcare for the day in Atlanta for my toddler daughter who would be traveling with me. Something within me told me that I needed to be there. I won't say that it changed my business, but I received a lot of good information. I also made some great connections.

Ultimately, though, I felt connected to the branding expert because I loved the fact that she showed up. She's significantly heavier than I am, and her courage and confidence motivated me. In spite of the cyberbullying she experienced, she would show up in excellence and with a full-blown expert attitude. Regardless of what people thought about her physical appearance, she knew that she was good at what she did and had something special to offer the world. I realize now that I went through the trouble to pull all of those strings, mainly because I wanted to support her, and on a second tier, to get what she had to offer. My close friend told me very blatantly she would not listen to this particular expert because she was overweight. In my friend's assessment, the expert's morbid obesity meant that there were other areas of her life that she did not have under control. Therefore, there was really nothing that she could teach my friend because the expert didn't even have herself together. I believe the total opposite. My friend demonstrated the very line of thinking that made me so afraid to put myself out there. My obesity stopped me from demonstrating my expertise and from sharing my creativity. It made me fear rejection. It made me question my worth. I believed that my weight was much louder and much more influential on people's opinion of me than my gifts and talents and as such would render them useless to those people. And in a sense, all of that was confirmed true for my friend. But the truth of the matter is my friend's opinion didn't influence me to not go and learn from this woman. It didn't influence the other women who were in the room of this sold-out intensive, nor the ones who chose to go with the upsell, which was thousands of dollars more, after the intensive. What she had to offer she knew was more valuable than what people perceived about her person. And she stood for that, addressed it head on, and allowed people to hold their opinions without sacrificing her purpose to them. That's what we're all called to do.

Do you have a crippling fear of rejection? Does it paralyze you and stop you from fulfilling your dreams and purpose? Does it stop you from showing up, from opening your mouth, from being visible, being present, being confident in the things that you know?

If you are clear on what you have to offer this world and if you go forward in that thing with all your heart, soul, mind, and passion, then people will align with your line of thinking and will galvanize to you. They will rally around you and will become your voice of defense like the Senior Class President did for me in that moment while I was on stage being booed. They will fight voraciously for you because of what you have offered to them, for the value that they believe you have and in spite of your flaws. Have you ever seen anyone being attacked by the Beyoncé fans online? Say anything negative about Beyoncé, and you will be swiftly swarmed with corrections and insults. Whether you're right or wrong in your assessment or observation, they form a barrier around their queen and protect her. God has a tribe for you, too. Your tribe will stand up for you and protect you from people's opinions, people's disruptions, and people's distractions. However, unless you open your mouth and give the world what you have, they won't know that that's their job to do. They won't have any motivation or incentive to rally around you because they won't even know that they are aligned with you.

My friend was not a part of the branding expert's tribe, but I was. What she represented, simply by showing up, was possibility. She gave me an opportunity to support her. In a sense, by supporting her, I was supporting the idea that I could show up and be successful, too, though it took me many more years to embrace that notion. Such confidence takes time and intentionality to build. And while the expert may have inherently possessed it, my confidence needed to be founded in Christ. My confidence had to be rooted in the unshakeable, unmovable, unchanging understanding of His unconditional love for me so that I could mirror that for myself and extend it to others as He commanded.

Your playing small doesn't help anyone but you. Actually, not even you. Consider your legacy. What will you leave your children and your children's children or simply the world (if you don't have children)? What will they say about you when you're gone? Will they know that you had a mission and you completed it? Or will they remember you as a dreamer who dreamed dreams and did not a thing? Wishing and planning but never executing and progressing cannot and will not be your legacy. Listen, the world is burning down all around you. You've got buckets of water, and you're not sharing. You're not sharing your solutions. You're not sharing your art. You're not sharing your voice. You're not sharing your heart. You're not sharing your gifts or your talents, and you're not fulfilling your purpose. Don't be deceived. No one is benefiting from that (especially not you)!

Believe me, I totally get that there is stress that comes with trials and tribulations. There's a refinement that occurs when you are put through the flames. You develop a tough outer shell when people's opinions stop mattering, and you see them for what they really are: worthless. Opinions don't change any of what God has determined and declared about you even before the dawn of time. Brené Brown shared a practice where she puts six names of the people closest to her and whose opinions matter most on a one-inch-by-one-inch notecard. She folds it up and keeps it with her. Whenever she's tempted to give weight to other people's opinions, she checks to see if those people's names are on that notecard. If they're not, she ignores them. That's some of the best advice that I've heard in a very long time. Trust the wise counsel of those who know you best, but even still, weigh them against what God has told you. Again, I think of Peter. When Jesus was telling Peter about His fate, Peter, undoubtedly from a place of love and positivity, told Jesus that, no, this terrible fate would not happen to Him. But Jesus rebuked him, saying,

"Get behind me, Satan!" I'm pretty sure that that wasn't the response Peter was expecting. That surely wasn't the response I was expecting. But eventually I understood that even your most well-meaning loved ones sometimes won't understand the call and purpose on your life. When it comes down to accepting or rejecting their well-meaning-but-contradictory-to-the-will-of-God advice, you must reject it with the same intensity as Christ.

For far too long, I have allowed the fear of rejection to stop me from fully living out my purpose. I've allowed the enemy to feed me lies about myself. This book is evidence of my growth and my efforts to allow the truth to set me free by unlearning those lies. What action can you take to counter the lies you've believed?

For Such a Time as This

I recently came across an Instagram post that quoted actress Danielle Brooks. In the post, she stated that she no longer sets New Year's resolutions because routinely, her resolutions would be centered around weight loss. She talked about how having such goals is superficial and not really what life's all about. She went on to share that she would usually set goals to stay under 200 pounds or to be out of double-digit sizes but came to realize as she got older that those things didn't matter. There were just better things to worry about in life. And I thank God for seeing that post, because in that moment, it was exactly what I needed to read and hear. I was on the struggle bus with my self-love that day. I was feeling inadequate. I was feeling stuck. More than likely, being on social media comparing myself was the main cause to these feelings, but at the right time, someone with an unpopular yet uplifting opinion slid into my perfection-filled feed and provided a safe space for people like me. So I smiled and said, "Thank you, God." I knew He was speaking to me through her. Then I went to the comment section. I knew better than to go to the comment section. But I scrolled anyway and came across negativity like this:

"It's all well and good until you get diabetes."

"Why settle for obesity?"

"Obesity isn't healthy, so even if you feel like you're healthy in two hundreds, you could be healthier."

My nostrils flared. My ears started to smoke. I felt personally attacked. I sat back and I frustratingly pondered this question: Why are we so worried about other people's sizes? Like, really, why are we so conditioned to be concerned with how big or small someone else is?

We've learned to make snap judgements about a person's size and conclude how she must live her life—with low self-esteem, lacking self-control, being lazy, not being very driven or accomplished. We surmise and dictate how overweight people must feel about themselves and encourage them to hate their imperfect bodies.

It made me really question why people get so offended by a bigger woman who decides that she's going to be happy while being bigger. We have adopted a culture of superficiality that makes us find our identity in how we look and teaches us to treat others based upon how they look. We preach about first impressions and impress upon people (women especially) that in order to achieve any level of success, they need to do the work. And that's true if you abide by the traditional idea of success. But at the pinnacle of that success, most come to find that after achieving and receiving everything that they were striving for that they are still discontent. It isn't enough. They realize that ultimately, they need to define success and every action necessary to achieve it, for themselves. I believe that's the point that Danielle may have reached when she made that decision and wrote that post. And that should have been enough. Yet instead, it was offensive because we, as human beings, like to box people in. We like for everyone to fit into neat little categories, neat little stereotypes. Having the audacity to embrace yourself at any size is somehow considered radical. Given the prevalence of diet culture, fitness crazes, and the bank-breaking medical industry, it's abundantly clear that if too many people became confident, then it would put a hole in a lot of pockets. It's the mindset that they're after.

I'm not saying people should be comfortable with being unhealthy. They should be uncomfortable with the fact that if there were no guilt or shame associated with being overweight, then some people would stand to lose a lot of money. There's an agenda that has been pushed for many, many years to get us to hate our flaws more than we love ourselves. We're obsessed with our size and not our overall well-being because we've been taught to be so that someone else can profit.

It's absolutely a mistake to make other people's acceptance your motivation. Beauty standards are fickle. We've gone from the thickness of Marilyn Monroe to the thinness of supermodels to the curviness of the Kardashians. They keep moving the goalposts. The game is designed to keep you in cycles and running in circles. It's designed to keep you discontent. You're never enough, according to culture. And if you don't know who you are and you accept that notion, then you will forever be striving to mold yourself into the popular, desired box of the ideal look. We shake our heads at the people who have gone too far—the Michael Jacksons, Lil Kims, Joan Riverses, and many, many other celebrities who have altered their faces and bodies. There are plenty of "regular" people who drink the Kool-Aid, though. There are people whom you know yet may not even realize are slipping down the path toward body dysmorphic disorder, bulimia, or anorexia, until it's too late. These conditions, diseases, and disorders were not God's plan for us.

When I was at my smallest weight, in my mind, I could have been smaller. At every point along my weight loss journey, the goal has always been to be smaller. I would cite wanting to be healthier or not wanting to develop diabetes as reasons for my obsession with my weight because that sounded good. These reasons sounded to others like I valued myself, when in reality, I was striving and obsessing because I believed losing the weight would make me valuable. I'll admit that when I am a smaller size, I am the most confident. I can't help but believe that when people look at me, they judge me to be smart, dedicated, pulled together, beautiful, and worthy of admiration when I am carrying less weight.

But as the saying goes, don't judge a book by its cover. You shouldn't judge a person by her exterior. Everything I possessed when I was smaller, I possess when I am bigger. The same can be said of many others. There's so much magnificence locked up inside of us, but we're unwilling to release it until we are physically worthy. Thankfully, the tide is starting to shift. I'm so glad there's a body positivity movement bubbling up. I am glad that retailers are jumping on the trend of offering cute curvy and plus-size fashions. There are more and more voices ringing out to question the status quo. Many others, like Danielle Brooks, are helping people accept themselves through their example.

Righting the ship may mean that you have to struggle fiercely with accepting yourself today as you are instead of chasing this carrot of weight loss. At some point, you have to hop off that hamster wheel and decide that "today, I'm going to simply accept me right where I am." Once you do, you can use that self-acceptance as your foundational point to make healthier choices, and if that leads to weight loss, that's fine, too.

I think it's time you stepped out and showed the people who watch and root for you that even while you're a work in progress, there is no need to be perfect to be present. They may not even know that that's what you're waiting for actually. Through transparently sharing your struggles, your humanity, you can inspire someone who has tricked herself into believing that she is alone to show up, too. We are all leaders; there is always someone who's watching and learning from us (whether they say it or not). So, if you hate or hate on yourself, you can have an effect on someone else who looks like you and looks up to you.

Sometimes your gifts and talents are the setup to get you through the door to fulfill your purpose. If Danielle Brooks had waited until she was an "acceptable" weight to start her acting career, she would not have achieved the success she has achieved that created the platform she has that enabled her to share the message that so blessed me that day. You don't know how your showing up in spite of your perceived flaws will position you to impact others in even more significant ways. Such was the case with Esther.

The Book of Esther in the Old Testament reads a lot like a soap opera, with all the deceit, betrayal, love, hate, death, and more permeating its pages. At its start, we find a merry and drunken King Xerxes giving an extended feast for everyone in his great kingdom. During the final day of these festivities, the king summons his beautiful queen, Vashti, to come and appear before him so he and his homeboys can gaze upon her beauty. The queen is throwing her own party, so she refuses and sets in motion a chain of events that makes this one of the most beloved stories in the Bible.

Enraged and embarrassed at her refusal, the king consults with his princes about what he should do about this disobedient queen. It is suggested according to the law that Vashti be cast out of the king's sight forever and replaced with a young virgin even more beautiful than she. (Is your inner feminist itching, too? Anyway...)

This proposal pleases the king, and that is that. A search is conducted, and after a year of preparation, many young beautiful women are brought before the king. He chooses Esther. Esther is a beautiful, young Jewish woman. She has a way of winning the favor and affection of anyone with whom she comes in contact. Undoubtedly, her beauty is a serious factor. But we come to learn that simply being a beautiful woman is not all Esther had going for her. She is humble and wise. She is brave and a risk taker. However, her greatest trait is her character.

Esther is crowned queen, but this is far from happily ever after. All the while, a subplot is forming. Haman, one of the king's princes, is plotting against the Jews all because Esther's cousin and guardian, Mordecai, refuses to bow before Haman as he passes by along the streets. Being haughty in character, this really upsets Haman. In fact, it makes him indignant enough to want to rid the world of not just Mordecai but all of Mordecai's people. So he sets out to do just that. He even goes so far as to get his scheme approved with an irreversible signature by way of the king's signet ring. With that, the Jews' annihilation becomes law.

All of the Jews are petrified. Mordecai puts on sackcloth, covers himself in ashes, and sits down outside the gates of the palace. When Esther hears about his behavior, she sends a servant to find out the reason he is mourning. He tells her the alarming news. He also instructs her to go into the presence of the king and to beg for the Jews' deliverance. Up until this point, on Mordecai's advice, Esther has not revealed her ethnic background to anyone. There's only one problem: no one can go before the king without first being summoned. If she does, and the king does not extend his scepter toward her, she will be put to death. Queen Esther relays this to Mordecai, and his reply is truly a motivational quote: "For if you remain silent at this time, relief and deliverance for the Jews will arise from another place, but you and your father's family will perish. And who knows but that you have come to your royal position for such a time as this?" (Esther 4:14, NLT).

Esther's purpose is revealed in that moment. Yet she does not jump right in. In the story, there is so much emphasis placed on time passing and preparation that it's only fitting that there be some passage of time and some type of preparation for what Esther is about to do. In her wisdom, she utilizes one of the most effective tools we have as believers: fasting. She asks her cousin Mordecai and the rest of the Jews to fast for three days. She and her maids fast as well.

Long story short: she goes before the king, and he lowers his scepter toward her. Her life is spared. With the wisdom she receives while fasting, she sets in motion her own plan to convince the king to also spare her people. Before the story is over, Esther wins the king's favor again and asks to create a new law that allows the Jews to defend themselves when the day comes for the other law to be fulfilled. She reveals Haman's true character, which results in the king having him killed. She also asks the king to kill Haman's sons (which is an ironic twist in that the family line of Haman is annihilated instead of the Jews). Mordecai gets elevated to Haman's position and receives all of his honors and wealth. Esther receives a holiday in her honor, and they all live happily ever after—or at least I'm going to assume so because the book ends there.

Secret Donuts

You should really go and read the entire book of Esther. There are so many lessons we learn from Esther's story. I think a major lesson is to get in position and to use that position the way that God would have you to. Esther, though beautiful and popular, remains humble and retains a teachable spirit. Though she has every reason to be, we are never led to believe that Esther is in the least bit self-absorbed.

Let's talk about the queen before Esther for a moment. Vashti was beautiful as queens are required to be, apparently. Not much else is shared about her character. I have often read the story and looked at the queen before Esther as the bad guy. She had one job: to show up and be beautiful. For so long, I held the belief that since she said "no," she deserved to lose her position. But as I matured, I started to look at it in a different way. Maybe this removal was a blessing in disguise for her. It's not clear how often she was asked and expected to stop everything that she was doing at the drop of a dime to go and be ogled at by the king and his boys. Maybe he disrespected her in other ways. Maybe she never wanted to be queen. I've always viewed the story with an emphasis on the position of "queen." But it's not really about the position at all. It's about purpose. It was Vashti's purpose to be removed from her position in that way. Who knows how long she would have remained queen? It's likely Mordecai never would have ever bowed before Haman, so an enraged Haman probably would have gone forward with his evil plot and God's people would have been destroyed. But because Vashti was removed and God elevated Esther at the right time, the Jews had a chance to be saved. Sometimes we find ourselves in rooms or sitting at tables we never would have imagined. We have to step up into leadership roles in ministry, parent children from a space of uncertainty, manage other people at work, or become the head of household when a parent passes away. It may be hard work. We may feel clueless and confused. It may seem scary or overwhelming. We might not even want the position, but the position puts us closer to our purpose. She wasn't out looking for a husband the day she was brought into the palace. Nevertheless Esther eventually became a queen. Esther's elevation allowed her to influence a king. That influence saved a nation.

So why are we talking about Esther anyway? In my mind, her charm and beauty opened many the doors, which kind of confirms the notion that people who look the part deserve the attention, position, power, love, respect, and more. Right? True. But there were still barriers to purpose and obedience that she had to overcome. The very thing that I have felt I am missing, the thing that would make everything easier and possible, is exactly what she had. But still, it wasn't enough. Not one quality you have is enough. It's not even enough if you have all the qualities. She needed God and she knew it. She fasted. She had all of the people fast, and when they finished their fast, she had courage and a plan. Even if we've got it all, we can't do it all in our own strength. Esther's story reminds me to put my faith in God, not in my looks.

10

Obedience Is Better, Trust Me

As believers, we are called to accept Jesus Christ as our Lord and Savior. A lot of us have mastered that "savior" part. It's with the "Lord" title that we often have issues. To most believers, it's not a comforting thought to let someone else lead and direct their every move (though we know that that is truly what we are called to do). Relinquishing control becomes an everyday struggle. We find ourselves unable to put things in God's hands, to let go, to let God, as we are so often encouraged by music and sermons. These controlling tendencies can be caused by fear. When we refuse to do something that God tells us to do because we fear of what might result, we are basically attempting to control the situation. A familiar example in Scripture is Jonah.

Was there ever an assignment that God gave you that you know was not going to have the outcome you wanted? Yet you felt this urge to continue to go through with it, right? Even worse, did you feel as though the mission that you were given was pointless? Jonah could relate. God instructed Jonah to go down to the great city of Nineveh and declare a message warning of the destruction they were facing because of their wickedness. Jonah decided that that was a mission impossible for him and instead fled from God on a boat in the opposite direction. His issue was not the fact that Nineveh was a very large city, one that took three days to cross by foot, nor was his issue that the people might react violently to his message. Instead, his fear was that once they received that message, the people of Nineveh would repent, and God would be gracious and have mercy, forgive them, and not follow through with his threat. This is exactly what happened, and Jonah was not pleased. In fact, he was so bitter about it that he asked God for death. Death.

Let's face it: Jonah was selfish. Imagine how magnificent of a preacher he had to be in order to bring an entire city and its leadership to repentance. Imagine being *that* gifted yet refusing to use it for God's will and purpose. Are you being selfish with your gifts and talents? Are you burying them because you know God's character? That he delivers on his promises? That he disciplines those he loves, which means that you were going to go through some tests, trials, and growing pains? Let's talk about burying talents and why it's not a good idea.

In Matthew, we find Jesus sharing yet another parable, this time about talents. The New International Version translates talents into "bags of gold." That's fitting because the gifts that God gives are even more valuable than that. In Jesus's story, a man going on a journey calls in his three servants and divides up his eight talents for them to take care of. He gives one of the men five talents, another two, and the last servant one. He makes his decision based on their individual abilities. The first two servants go and double their portions, but the last guy buries his talent in the ground. He does this because he is afraid and he believes he serves a hard and seemingly unfair man. Well, as you can probably guess, when he returns, the master is pretty pleased with the first two, singing their praises and giving them more talents to manage. He gleefully invites them to share in his happiness. The third guy? Well, he is called some pretty harsh names like "wicked" and "lazy," reprimanded, and stripped of his talent, only to watch it be given to his coworker with the most. Then he is thrown out into the bitter darkness!

No matter how you feel about it, God has given you talents based on your ability and expects you to go out and be fruitful with them. Invest in your talents and then invest your talents. Take time to sharpen your ability so that as much fruit as possible can be produced from them. Take your talents, and whether you have been given a huge task or a small one, execute it with wisdom and integrity so that you can hear "Well done, my good and faithful servant."

You have to have a servant's heart if you're going to serve the Lord. Once you accept the Lord, you have to also accept the fact that you are no longer the king or queen of your life. In fact, you never were. You are now and have always been a slave. Paul tells us in Romans 6:17-18 (NLT), "But thanks be to God that, though you used to be slaves to sin, you have come to obey from your heart the pattern of teaching that has now claimed your allegiance. You have been set free from sin and have become slaves to righteousness." Before you accepted Jesus into your life, you were a slave to the evil and wicked ways of the world and the evil and wicked ways of yourself, yet now that you have turned away and into the care of the Lord, you are better off if you let him do just that: care for you. By doing so, you become a slave to righteousness. You surrender yourself in service to God's will and purpose.

If you understand that his knowledge and wisdom are above your own, then what good is it to continue to try to figure things out on your own? Are you worried about the future? God is there, right now, while you are worried, observing what is happening. With His foresight, He is able to give you instructions for the present time that relate to what He sees in the future right now. Even if you are like Jonah and can guess pretty accurately from experience what might happen, don't argue with God about it, because He may be using this assignment as a teachable moment much like he did with Jonah. Because Jonah was finally obedient we, from reading his experience, learn that God is gracious and merciful.

"Do you see a man who is good at his work? He will stand in front of kings. He will not stand in front of men who are not important." —*Proverbs 22:29, NLV*

Tricia Smith Brown is an event planner whom I found and followed on Instagram some years ago. Talk about business goals. The only word that comes to mind when she recaps her work is "excellent." She excels. She takes the talent that God clearly gave her and multiplies it. Her passion shows and inspires. I always leave her page thinking, "I can do better. I can push further." And I am convinced that though we are not in the same industry, we *can* share the same characteristics. Passion. Focus. Discipline. Consistency. Excellence.

I've always loved Proverbs 22:29. It's a great reminder to always give it your all. But one thing I had to learn is that when you are good, you are *able* to stand in front of anyone, but you get to *choose* to stand in front of "kings" and important people. Being excellent provides you with options.

I love the part of the verse that says that the man is good at his work. I believe that's an important distinction: his work. In my opinion, his work doesn't just mean he's simply mastered a trade, but that he's mastered a trade *and* his personal way of doing it. Just like with Tricia Smith Brown, I am sure that there are plenty of wonderfully gifted event planners who can do what she does, but they don't do it in the way she does. She's found her work and gotten good at doing it.

When you focus on getting good at your work, you will be more fulfilled. You will find that the things that you were trying to use your work to obtain—which could include the money, success, stunting, attention, and accolades—become the byproducts of it when you pursue it in excellence. They become a reality because the right people will start to notice the special thing that you have to offer. "Let your work move you forward" is a quote I internalized the first time I watched and listened to a speech given by Ava Duvernay. For many years, whenever I have gotten off track, I have come back to this quote and it has grounded me. Nothing and *no one* (outside of God) can move you forward faster than your work if you are working to get good, staying focused, and staying real.

A word of caution: though you are pursuing excellence, don't get wrapped up in doing it "right." Remember, excellence should not be confused with perfection. Perfection is a myth; a lie designed to keep your heart discontent and your creativity stifled. Excellence is pursuing and executing your personal best (without comparing it to anyone else). Your pursuit of excellence should originate with your pursuit of God. Your motivation to perform well should be the respect that you have for the gifts and talents God has given you. Be like the servants who went and doubled their bags of gold. Remember *why* you do what you do and do it to the best of your ability and in a way that makes your heart full.

Gideon, Esther, and Jonah are three of my favorite people from the Bible. They have very interesting stories. I used them as examples here because although their circumstances, talents, assignments, and attitudes varied, the attributes of God remain constant in all three accounts. That's important to know because no matter what God has called you to do, no matter how much your assignment and purpose differ from what He has called other women to, we can all depend on the same promises from an unchanging God. His promises are yes and amen. The more we learn about Him, the truer it becomes in our hearts. He rains down grace and mercy, wisdom and knowledge. He gives meaning to our short days on Earth. We can't spend the majority of those days waiting on some level of physical "perfection" that He hasn't even asked us to attain. Let Him ease that burden. Put Him back on the throne in place of your pride and ego. We should all humble ourselves with the understanding of who God is and the importance of His will being done and His purpose coming to pass on this Earth as it is in heaven.

Following the instructions of Matthew 6:33 liberates us from the fear, guilt, shame, and other children of sin that hold us captive while fervently seeking things other than God. Shifting our focus to pursuing God empowers us to move in the strength that we have, in the bodies that we have, in the knowledge that we have, and with the resources that we have. It gives us confidence to know that God will do what we can't and through us He will receive the glory. It is my hope that this section allowed you to get a clearer view of God and an understanding of the importance of His will and purpose so that we can begin pursuing health from a space of understanding who God is and how much He loves us every minute of every day regardless of how we look, how we feel, or any other condition.

If it has, then let's move on to the next section. There I will offer some practical advice, resources, and insight about how we can start to incorporate healthier habits and continue to change our mindset around weight loss (keeping God at the forefront). I'm not a doctor, nor do I play one on TV. As with any lifestyle change, it's important to always seek the advice of your physician or other qualified healthcare provider with any questions you may have about a medical condition or treatment and before making any changes to your diet or exercise regimen.

PART III

From God's Love to Self-Love

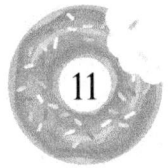

Do You See These Gains?

There's a popular meme going around. It reads, "Don't let the internet rush you." It's such a great reminder. I follow quite a few fitness-based accounts, and every time I scroll past a new picture from one of them, it makes me feel like I need to get up and run a few miles. When I see their hard-earned results, banging bodies, and befores and afters, I feel like I am really far behind. And in essence, I am. Those ladies are probably leaps and bounds ahead of me mentally. They got clear enough to be able to love and care for their bodies enough to say "enough" and make drastic and lasting changes.

Here's the thing though: there's no deadline on this. The weight loss rations won't run out. I have received a "no" for now simply because I am not ready, but I had to rest in the fact that when time came for me to lose weight, God would provide a peace-filled and spirit-led way to do so. I have lost weight in the past, sometimes without it even being the focus, like when I picked up a new sport or did a corporate fast with my church. Other times, I intentionally found a diet that worked or exercised consistently for long enough to see some changes. But those results haven't been lasting results. My lifestyle hadn't changed in the way I needed to maintain those results because my mindset needed to be addressed first.

The first thing I had to acknowledge was that negative self-talk is counterproductive. We can't shame ourselves into losing weight in a healthy way. We are not what we do. There's a difference between saying "I am fat" and "I've done something that will make me fat." There's a difference between thinking "I have no self-control" and admitting "I did not control myself." One denotes hopelessness and powerlessness. The other reinforces the understanding that you have power over your choices and that you can control your actions if you are aware, determined, and intentional. Replacing your bad habits with good habits begins with belief, good thoughts, and positive affirmations. One of the most positive affirmations of which I remind myself often is Psalm 139:1-18 (NLT):

1   You have searched me, Lord,
      and you know me.
2   You know when I sit and when I rise;
      you perceive my thoughts from afar.
3   You discern my going out and my lying down;
      you are familiar with all my ways.
4   Before a word is on my tongue
      you, Lord, know it completely.

Secret Donuts

5   You hem me in behind and before,
     and you lay your hand upon me.
6   Such knowledge is too wonderful for me,
     too lofty for me to attain.
7   Where can I go from your Spirit?
     Where can I flee from your presence?
8   If I go up to the heavens, you are there;
     if I make my bed in the depths, you are there.
9   If I rise on the wings of the dawn,
     if I settle on the far side of the sea,
10 even there your hand will guide me,
     your right hand will hold me fast.
11 If I say, "Surely the darkness will hide me
     and the light become night around me,"
12 even the darkness will not be dark to you;
     the night will shine like the day,
     for darkness is as light to you.
13 For you created my inmost being;
     you knit me together in my mother's womb.
14 I praise you because I am fearfully and wonderfully made;
     your works are wonderful,
     I know that full well.
15 My frame was not hidden from you
     when I was made in the secret place,

when I was woven together in the depths of the earth.
16 Your eyes saw my unformed body;
all the days ordained for me were written in your book
 before one of them came to be.
17 How precious to me are your thoughts, God!
How vast is the sum of them!
18 Were I to count them,
they would outnumber the grains of sand—
when I awake, I am still with you.

That passage of scripture is everything. Seriously, it embodies the majority of what I needed to learn and what I am expressing with this book. God is and has always been with us, He knows us intimately, and He created us the way He created us on purpose and for a purpose. We are significant. We are known. So now our focus from that point of understanding should be a journey to learn and know ourselves as God knows us. In essence, we need to take all the days that He's allotted for us and grow into the people that He envisioned us being by the end of it all.

There came a pivotal point when I stopped worrying about how much I was losing and became more interested in how I was growing. You will be able to lose weight with an unhealthy mindset, but a healthy mindset won't be dependent upon how much weight you lose, how you look, or any other external factors.

Secret Donuts

Eventually I began to proclaim that I wanted to be the fittest and healthiest I've ever been. I meant internally and externally. Simply setting a goal of being smaller and weighing less didn't deal with the body image or self-worth issues I had. Therapy, coupled with spiritual growth, understanding that I am known, that I'm fearfully and wonderfully made, and that I am a part of God's plan has been far more life defining than a physical transformation alone could have ever been. It has been so reassuring and liberating to embrace the fact that even when I'm not perfect, I am purposed. There is a reason for me to be here, and is not just to be fit and sexy. This is a counter-cultural perspective, especially for women. We can't go to a holiday gathering without an aunt, mother, grandmother, or cousin commenting on our weight or monitoring what goes on our plates. And while they are well meaning, there's so much more to us.

Daily affirmations might help to counter the voices in your head and the lingering voices of culture, media, and loved ones that try to convince you that you aren't enough or that you should feel guilt or shame about your weight. "Catch it. Check it. Change it." is a simple quote I learned from a wise woman named April Goodwin. When negative thoughts begin to float through your mind, do just that. Be aware of the lies of the enemy. Check what you're thinking against the truth of God. And if it doesn't align, change it. Watch what you say and think about yourself. Be as nice to yourself as you would a close friend.

We have to back it up a bit, though. How can you replace your thoughts if you have nothing to replace them with? You need quiet time with God and His Word. That way, you can build a reserve of positive, truth-filled alternatives to the thoughts that keep you captive. Instead you can take control of your thoughts with the power you receive from embracing and filling yourself up with the Word of God. 2 Corinthians 10:5 says, "We demolish arguments and every pretension that sets itself up against the knowledge of God, and we take captive every thought to make it obedient to Christ" (NIV).

They say that an idle mind is the devil's workshop. Every time you're bored or tempted to scroll aimlessly on social media, read some scripture, watch a sermon, pray, journal, and fill your mind with good things. Even while scrolling aimlessly, we are being exposed to thoughts and ideas that we didn't previously hold. The more we see and read that idea, the truer it becomes for us. During those times, don't give Satan a foothold or a path in. Inevitably when you open a social app, you'll see something that will influence your mood (whether good or bad). However, as we are working to change our perspective, the only influence we want is God's. Fill up and even put a wall up if necessary. If you need to take a break from social media (and even from being social) in order to ensure that God's voice is the loudest that you hear, then do just that.

Feel Great, Look Great

One of the biggest realizations that I've had to date is that with every day that passes, I am the "me" of the future that I have been holding out for. I don't look anything like I imagined, but look at me, being and such. The more time I hold out for a better me, the more time I lose. The more I hold out for a better me, the more life experience I miss out on. How unnecessarily devoid of joy and abundance is that—and by no one's fault but my own. I am withholding it from myself, waiting for an acceptable version of me to arrive. Yet I am currently that version of me that I have to accept. This is some *Inception*-type stuff, but I hope you're staying with me. Quite simply, until I embrace the version of Alicia I am now, the version of Alicia that I have been holding out for, the one I have been hoping for, won't ever show up. She already has everything I am withholding from the present me, so if I would just give those things to the present me, then I would be able to become the version of me that I have been hoping for all along.

I don't think I am alone or unique when I say this. I know you feel it. One way that this idea manifests is in how I dress. I have this problem with shopping. I don't do it. I always tell my husband he is blessed because he has a wife who doesn't spend all of the money on clothes and shoes. But my bragging would dry up as soon as I would run into the dilemma of never having anything to wear.

I have developed the habit of buying cheap clothes, reasoning that it would be unwise to invest in clothes because I was going to lose 80 pounds by next month. It would be a waste of money to buy lots of clothes at "this size" because I didn't plan to stay this size. But months and years have gone by, and I've often found myself frustrated while getting ready to go to an event. I would be ripping my closet apart trying to find something to wear, usually unsuccessfully. I also developed a habit of repeating just a few items until they were worn out. Sometimes, I would grow sick of them (and my husband would, too). These few items looked good on me or felt comfortable. But instead of buying more of them or items similar to them, I would revert to the mindset that I shouldn't invest. So in addition to not feeling great in my skin, I wasn't even feeling great in what I put over my skin. My inner frumpiness was translating to outer frumpiness.

As I mentioned earlier in this book, shopping was traumatic for me. I don't go shopping with friends and do little fashion shows in the dressing rooms. My shopping trips are more need based than fun or enjoyable. I never developed a passion for fashion. I don't really have an excuse for frumpiness these days, though, because there are so many brands that are specifically for plus sizes and others that have plus lines. On social media, you can find fashion accounts and brands with great examples of how to recreate looks from top to bottom. Yet I have still had apprehension. I'd look at these beautiful heavier women slaying with confidence and would think, "Good for them. But I don't want to dress up this body. I don't want to slay at this size. I don't want to settle." I've been waiting until I could slay with no bumps and jiggles and no shapewear. Yep, I've been waiting. And waiting and waiting.

When you look good, you feel good. I am a creative, so I can pull a cute outfit together if I really want to. But most days, I haven't really wanted to. There are days when I dress up and feel really good. But I have to be honest—on those same days, I can leave the house feeling one way but jump into a picture and after I look at it, feel really deflated. The angles they captured weren't the angles I saw in the mirror before I left the house. And before I left the house, I didn't pose next to a smaller beautiful lady (where I would look bigger by comparison).

I know this experience is not unique to me. But hear me when I say this: life is too short to wait to live it. Don't wait to adorn your body. You have not settled if you choose to love and adorn your body now, right where you are. Fashion, shopping, and getting cute are not a privilege of thin people. It's for us, too. Today. Right now. Part of changing the negative mindset is also changing the negative behaviors, so start being positive about and doing positive things for your body. Start with figuring out your body type and learning what looks good on you. Consult a stylist or a personal shopper so that you can get an unbiased set of eyes on your fashion situation. Invite her to evaluate your closet, then begin to fill it with things you love and in which you can be confident. Set yourself up to win. The shift won't happen overnight, but with consistency and by capturing your thoughts and exchanging them for positive, possibility-filled ones, you can make strides.

Seriously, you have to find what works for you. I say this from experience. I recently attended an event in Maryland hosted by the brand Ten. It was an absolutely amazing experience. It was the complete opposite of everything about shopping that gave me anxiety in the past. There were fewer shoppers (fewer than 20), which worked well for me because I am an introvert. There was a beautiful decor and a chill atmosphere with places to sit and fellowship with other shoppers. There was food. There were gift boxes for each attendee. And of course, there were clothes and accessories. And everything was affordable (because they believe that "Paying full price is a sin"). What made it great was that it wasn't overwhelming. There were only a few racks. But there was a nice selection of things in my size and only cute things. It was like having a personal stylist. I had too many options, which was a new experience for me. As I stood in the dressing room, trying on item after item, nearly everything fit. Nearly everything looked great. And even while I was in there, the host was pulling other items from the back for me (without me even asking) that she thought I would love and would look good on me. In the end, I had to narrow it down, but everything I bought, I was excited to wear. I vowed to the host that I would never shop in the traditional way ever again.

This is new to me in that, one, I was even open to go to a shopping event like this, and two, I found a whole new way to shop that I love. It was a win-win because I went to show support and walked away with so much value. With assistance, I was able to adorn myself with clothing I like. I made it to an event (which is a big flipping deal as an introvert). I even gleefully allowed them to photograph me (another big deal), and I didn't immediately tear myself apart (as much) when reviewing the picture (still working on this). I also made some new connections. Moreover, it never occurred to me before this that I could allow other people to operate in their gifting in this area and really bless me. This experience made my life so much richer. And to think I would have skipped it because I had been honed in on my size and weight. This is not a plug or an advertisement, but I want to give honor where it's due. I also share so that you might be able to open your mind up, too. If you can't get to Maryland, there may be something similar in your area. You might even enjoy an online personal shopping service. There are several out there; do a bit of research to see what's available.

Ultimately, the point is to remind you (and myself) not to put life on hold until we figure this weight thing out. Live life, enjoy life, love people, and pursue purpose today, right now while you (we) still have time. The reality is that no one knows the day or hour we'll check out of here. We don't have time to waste wishing and waiting. We should definitely be spending that time loving, learning, and living.

I've finally gotten to the point where I actually can love my body like this, not in the superficial way, like when you say "I love this song" or "I love that store," but unconditionally, like with the same love you extend to your spouse. If you think about it, you *are* with your body for life. Through sickness and health, for richer or poorer, through good times and bad times. Your body's not going anywhere, so you might as well treat it right. And guess what—if you treat it right, it will more than likely treat you right. You'll be very happy together.

I don't always love how I look, but I love my body. I'm grateful for it, flaws and all. I am thankful for all that it can do. I'm thankful for what it has done. It has been harmed and healed, persevering through colds, the flu, chicken pox, workouts, slips and falls, allergic reactions, physical fights, car accidents, and more. It has carried two little lives and has survived the trauma of childbirth. It moves, pops, and sways rhythmically when I have dance-offs in the kitchen with my daughter. It keeps up effortlessly when I chase down and rescue my son on his bike. It reacts and responds to danger before I even have a chance to think about it. It fills with adrenaline and sends power to my legs in case I want to "fight or flight" a spider. Yes, my body has been good to me.

Secret Donuts

Loving your body means wanting the best for it. It means doing all you can to take care of it because it's the only body you have and will get in this life. And just like any other relationship, it takes intentionality, work, and effort to maintain it. Embrace that. It's obvious and almost goes without saying that your body is yours. You have the ability to grow, nurture, and nourish it. You have so much power to change it and shape it. You have the responsibility to do what's beneficial for it. The trick is moving from *needing* to wanting to.

Work out because you love yourself. Eat healthier because your body is important and you want to fuel it. Create a self-care routine because you value your life and know you're worth it. Discipline yourself because you know that it's best; don't use it as some kind of punishment or as an end to a means.

With that in mind, how are you conditioning your body? Are you moving it? Are you putting your exercise on the backburner for more important things? There are deadlines to meet. Hungry kids who need to be fed. Your husband needs your attention. Your aging parents need your assistance. Your friends need your shoulder. And after a long day, you just want to relax on the couch. Or are you the opposite? You stay up far past your bedtime to get everything done. You know the saying: you can't pour from an empty cup. Don't fall apart trying to hold it all together.

Many people who live life in that way often end up with regrets when the time comes to pay up for that lifestyle. Again, no one knows the time or place when they will die.

And everyone has got to go. So why not try to enjoy life? You can't stop the inevitable. This is true. But I would think that with knowing the brevity of life, you would be more inclined to get the most out of it. I'm intent on using this life I have been given to make an impact on myself and others. I want to live like I am dying. I want to experience all of the abundance that God has promised me, even if that means being uncomfortable (like by being told to not lose weight for an entire year). The whole point of this book is getting over your weight and into your purpose. We can tackle that first part mentally, but there is absolutely a physical component. Once you know how to love and value yourself properly, you'll feel the responsibility to take care of your body physically because your mission and purpose are too important.

My daughter is living my childhood Barbie collection fantasy right now. She has tons of dolls and accessories, two houses, three cars, a jet plane, a horse stable, and more. Naturally, I have more of a vested interest in her taking care of every single Barbie-related piece, down to the smallest pair of pink cat-eye sunglasses. I insist that she takes care of all the pieces not only out of respect to us, because everything she has was gifted to her, but because I know how much more fun and creative her playtime is when she has everything in its place and in working order. Our bodies were gifted to us by God. We can treat them any way we want to, but out of respect to our creator, we really should take better care of them. Additionally, we know that caring for ourselves gives us a chance at a more abundant life—one devoid of the stress of dealing with preventable health issues. We know that when we are more like Jesus, part of that calls for us to deny the permissible for what's more beneficial, or even better, to deny the permissible for obedience. We love the giver more than the gift, but we love the gift because of who gave it.

They say if you stay ready, you don't have to get ready. The question becomes: for what are we staying ready? Think of it like a basketball team. There are five players on the court at any given time. There are also seven players on the bench. Those benched players may not be starters, but they are prepared to enter the game when the coach gives the word. When they enter the game, they need to have the same stamina, skills, and knowledge of the playbook as the starters. We can view our care for our bodies in the same way. We should take care of ourselves because we love ourselves as God loves us. We should also take care of ourselves so that we can stay physically ready to carry out the mission that God has assigned to us. When He calls us up off the bench, we need to be ready.

The Apostle Paul gives us another sports analogy, saying, "Don't you realize that in a race everyone runs, but only one person gets the prize? So run to win! All athletes are disciplined in their training. They do it to win a prize that will fade away, but we do it for an eternal prize. So I run with purpose in every step. I am not just shadow boxing. I discipline my body like an athlete, training it to do what it should. Otherwise, I fear that after preaching to others I myself might be disqualified" (1 Corinthians 9:24-27, NLT).

So then, "Physical training is good, but training for godliness is much better, promising benefits in this life and in the life to come" (1 Timothy 4:8, NLT). I'm not saying that physical appearance doesn't matter. I just mean to say that we should want to look good because we love ourselves (and not only love ourselves because we look good). That love for ourselves will be derived from our understanding of God's love for us. And from that knowledge, we find the motivation to love and take care of ourselves because we are so valuable to Him first and foremost.

Let's start here: we were not designed to be sedentary. I'm sure that you've heard by now that there are physical, physiological, and mental benefits to working out. Maybe you've tried working out in the past, though, and nothing you did actually worked out for your weight loss.

I recommend that you stop trying to find something that works and start seeking God. Invite Him into your decision-making by asking Him what would be best for you. He can show you ways to get fit that you may not have ever even thought of. I had a coworker who lost weight simply by buying a new house. The new house was multilevel and newer and nicer than the one she was leaving. Once they were all moved in, she spent a lot more time up on her feet moving about, going up and down stairs and cleaning up her house. She wanted to keep it nice and maintain it, and an added benefit to that was that she ended up losing weight in the process. Unintentionally, it became regular physical activity, and after seeing such great results, she started to incorporate exercise into her daily life. She found things that she liked to do, she invited other people to do it with her, and she set goals for herself. That motivated her to change her diet. She lost weight slowly but surely. I found this to be very inspiring and very comforting as well. Beginning to exercise didn't have to be a big production. You could start out so simply and still see results. You just have to keep up the momentum.

The time of the day that you work out may matter. You may need to start your day with the workout to make sure that you don't have to find time to do it later. We have a tendency to put ourselves last and on the back burner. So if working out before you start your day guarantees that you'll get it done, go ahead and put yourself first. Working out in the morning sets the tone for the rest of your day. The sense of accomplishment and release of endorphins may better prepare you to handle the rest of your day with a more positive attitude and perspective.

I have personally found that instead of winding down on the couch watching television after my kids go to bed, it has been much more relaxing and beneficial to end my day at the gym. At that hour, there are fewer people sharing the equipment, I can relax after my workout by taking advantage of the spa amenities that come with my membership, and I can take my time because there's nothing to do afterwards. Whatever you do, do what will allow you to stay consistent. They say if you do what you love, it'll feel like you've never worked a day in your life or you'll never have to work another day in your life. I feel the same about exercise. If you find something that you love to do, it won't feel like you're exercising. The experience will overshadow the pain. There are many ways to get your heart rate up, to take care your your body, to build it and shape it into what you want to be. Park further away from the door when shopping. Take the stairs. Take a walk around the block at home or at work. Get some Air Monarchs and take a walk around the mall. Get a bike and go for a ride with your kids. Go dance. Or dance at home. Listen: find a wedding reception playlist. You can cupid shuffle and cha cha slide your way into fitness, right at home. Seriously, just find something you love and do that. You don't need a gym membership (I actually hate the gym, too), but you can find all kinds of fitness videos on YouTube. There are hundreds of thousands of workouts shared on there. Or you can download a personal training app on your phone. Make a Pinterest board with lifting routines or 30-day challenges. Buy a jump rope. Create your own in home gym. You can fill it with everything you need and decorate it in whatever way will motivate you to spend time in the space. Get a personal trainer. Take classes (like kickboxing). Join group fitness boot camp. Join a running club. Train for a 5K, half marathon, or triathlon. Sign up for a fitness competition if you need to press toward a goal or you like to compete and win. Join a competition for a cash prize (like Runbet/Dietbet) and let the investment motivate you. Join a recreational league or team (baseball, basketball, kickball, softball) and relive your glory days. Get an accountability group together so you have someone to check up on and push (read: annoy) you. Use your technology. You can track your progress through apps or natively on your phone. Just make time for you. Increase your chances of consistency by doing things that you enjoy, not hate. And if you need to set a goal to lose weight so that you have some milestones to hit, that's fine, too.

However, if I were you, I would avoid the scale like the plague. Why? It's a myth that muscle weighs more than fat, but by volume, muscle takes up less space and is less dense. So, you can look different but weigh the same on the scale. Sometimes it's hard to see a physical change in ourselves because we look at ourselves daily. So the scale staying the same might make you feel like all of the work you did was in vain. Instead, in order to stay encouraged, find different ways to track your progress. Take and record your measurements on a schedule. Pay attention to how you feel. Has your brain fog disappeared? Do you feel stronger? More energetic? Are you in a better mood overall? Take before pictures and update them every week or month. Buy a pair of goal jeans and track your process by how they fit. Pay attention to how all of your clothes feel. Are they looser and more comfortable? Is it time to go shopping because you're now swimming in them? These are just a few ways to track your progress; I am sure there are many more ways. The important thing to remember is that the number on the scale or the size on your tag tells only a fraction of the story of your journey.

Since we're over guilt and shame, let me just add another reminder right here. Don't be embarrassed if you jiggle when you run, break a sweat more quickly than you'd like, or have to take it slow to start because you get very winded very easily. Don't be intimidated by women who have six packs and peach-shaped glutes. Remember, they had to start somewhere, too. And in reality, fewer people are looking at or judging you than you think. Most are probably applauding you in their minds because you're making a change that they think you ought to. Either way, their opinions don't matter. You're doing this for you. You're doing this for God. You're making changes to be more fit to fulfill your purpose (and you'll reap the benefits that come with it). Keep your "why" at the forefront of your mind so that when negative and discouraging thoughts pop up, you can combat them with the truth.

Even if you're not looking to lose weight at the moment, regular exercise increases your overall quality of life. It's time for you to stop hiding. Get up and get out. Show up and show your face. Enjoy life. Physical activities are for you, too.

These Snacks Ain't Loyal

So, we've reached the worst part of the book for me. But don't fret, because it's also the best part. It's the final level—my King Koopa; the opponent I need to defeat to win the whole game. It's like the last Infinity Stone and we've been gaining power like Thanos throughout our entire journey of this book. (Can you tell that I have a brother and a son?) It has not been easy, and this part is probably going to take all the determination we have, all of the discipline we can stand, and all the commitment we can muster. But when we *finally* get through this part, we will have an indescribable freedom. Chains will fall off. The gates will swing open. The princess will finally be saved. (See what I did there? Princess? We're God's daughters—never mind).

We'll start with the truth: letting go of food is hard. We celebrate with food. It nourishes. It comforts. It's vital for life. And bottom line: it tastes amazing. You know I'm not talking about all food right now though. I'm talking about the foods that may not necessarily serve us but they are the foods that we were served. It's what we know. There are memories attached to dishes like Granny's sweet potato pies or the greasy snacks you shared with dad on game day. It's the holiday foods that we eat on non-holidays. I'm unintentionally raising a baked macaroni and cheese connoisseur myself, and best believe, she judges people and restaurants hard on the subject. It's the quick and simple drive-thru solution to a busy night with the kids after a crazy day at work. And tomorrow evening's solution and also Friday's solution. (Don't worry, I'm just putting myself on blast.)

In moderation, they may be fine. But we aren't moderating. Let me speak for myself: I haven't been moderating. I definitely have approached each day with good intentions. I would think to myself that today would be the day that I make the change. I might even go as far as to meal plan. I might go even further and meal prep. But when mealtime rolled around and that hunger hit me in the depths of my belly, the last thing I wanted was something green or some reheated chicken that I cooked three days ago. No, in that moment I would want something yummy, something satisfying, something that would hit the spot just right. And in that moment I would habitually declare out loud that I didn't care if it was the right choice right before I grabbed it. "I likes ya, and I wants ya!" I'd say (to pizza).

Three things I have avoided like the plague: denial, deprivation, and discomfort. They've always felt so much like self-abuse. If I loved myself, why would I inflict such pain and suffering upon myself? Why would I sit there and drool while my coworkers enjoyed cupcakes and pizza? If I am feeling down, why wouldn't I eat half a pan of brownies and soothe? If I have a birthday, why wouldn't I invite my friends and family out to my favorite restaurant? Don't I deserve sparkler candles and an off-key random birthday song from the waitstaff? If this cruel, cruel world is not going to celebrate me, I for dang-sure will take care of myself. Treating myself is self-care. At least it feels like it is. The reality, though, is that the three things I've been avoiding are just components of discipline. And discipline is the unsung hero of self-care. If self-care is what we are truly seeking, we will have to master discipline.

Do you remember watching *The Maury Show* in the late 90s and 2000s? They aired a recurring show topic that I loved when I was a petty, messy teenager. Before they would bring the guest on stage, they would play her setup video. It would go something like this:

Cue dramatic music with heavy percussion. Quick pan and zoom in

"Maury, my name is Jessica, and I don't care what people say, I'm a good mom! I feed my baby three pancakes, four bowls of cereal, one brownie, a glass of chocolate milk, a glass of orange juice, four pieces of fried chicken, a waffle, some Cheetos, a Snickers bar, and two liters of orange soda. And that's just for breakfast! And guess what? I'll do it all again for lunch because I LOVVVVE MY BABY."

Then Jessica and her 137-pound two-year-old would enter the stage to a chorus of cheesy talk show music and the crowd booing. I would join in on the judgement, side-eyeing

Jessica so hard that my eyeballs could roll around the back and to the other side of my head. Because anyone with any good sense (even those who watched *The Maury Show* on a regular basis) would know that allowing that baby to eat that much of that kind of food was borderline child abuse. It didn't matter how much she claimed to love him. That's just not how you take care of a baby.

Sensible parents know kids need balanced meals. We know that being overweight is dangerous for their overall health. We want them to be able to run and jump and play without issues, like kids should. We don't want them to stand out or to be teased. I think the main reason that people were judgmental of Jessica is that ultimately, a child that young depends on his mom to make the right and responsible decisions for him. She is the one with authority over his diet. She has to be wise and deny him what he wants sometimes, even if he screams, kicks, and cries. It's her responsibility to use her authority as a parent to do better because she is the one who knows better.

With that in mind, when it comes to making healthier choices, we have to parent ourselves like we would parent our own children. We are God's children after all. We have to pipe up and say "No" to ourselves. We have to let "Because I said so!" shut down the argument about French fries over salad.

We have been given free will and authority over ourselves. We are free. We can do what we want. Every January, all across America, churches declare a corporate Daniel Fast.

Secret Donuts

It's based on the Biblical character, Daniel, who became a captive of Nebuchadnezzar, the King of Babylon, when he came to Jerusalem and besieged it. The king told the chief of his court officials to "bring into the king's service some of the Israelites from the royal family and the nobility—young men without any physical defect, handsome, showing aptitude for every kind of learning, well informed, quick to understand, and qualified to serve in the king's palace." Daniel was among them. In Chapter 1 Verse 5 NLT , we learn that "The king assigned them a daily amount of food and wine from the king's table. They were to be trained for three years, and after that they were to enter the king's service." I find Verse 8 particularly interesting, though: "But Daniel resolved not to defile himself with the royal food and wine, and he asked the chief official for permission not to defile himself this way."

Most people would gladly eat the royal food and drink the royal wine without a second thought. Daniel saw the royal food and wine as defiling rather than an opportunity to indulge. To defile means: desecrate or profane (something sacred) or sully, mar, or spoil. Desecrate means: treat (a sacred place or thing) with violent disrespect; violate.

Wow. Have you ever looked at food and determined it to be violently disrespectful to your body? I've had foods that were violently disrespectful to my taste buds (hello, liver), but that's a matter of opinion. What Daniel was feeling was deep seated, nearly anxiety inducing, and so much so that he had to speak up. But here's the other piece: I've never truly viewed my body as something sacred. Important? Yes. Sacred?

No. What does sacred mean? It's to be "connected with God (or the gods) or dedicated to a religious purpose and so deserving veneration (great respect or reverence)." It's true that we've been reminded time and again that our bodies are a temple through scripture and preachers. But how many of us seriously embrace this view?

Daniel faced some opposition from the chief official when he asked for permission to not eat the royal food and wine.

Now God had caused the official to show favor and compassion to Daniel, but the official told Daniel, "I am afraid of my lord the king, who has assigned your food and drink. Why should he see you looking worse than the other young men your age? The king would then have my head because of you" (Daniel 1:9-10, NLT).

One "no" didn't deter him. It was important enough for Daniel to keep pursuing, so he went to the guard that the chief official had appointed over him saying, "Please test your servants for ten days: Give us nothing but vegetables to eat and water to drink. Then compare our appearance with that of the young men who eat the royal food, and treat your servants in accordance with what you see" (Daniel 1:12-13, NLT). He agreed, and at the end of the ten days, he found that Daniel and his three friends looked healthier and better nourished than any of the young men who ate the royal food. So the guard took it away and put everyone on a diet of vegetables and water.

Up until that point, the king and his officials thought that this was the only way to eat in order to be fit enough to carry out the king's mission. They were after the results, not the actual diet, so much so that the official feared for his life. But Daniel went against their culture to prove to them that his way of eating would be even better. He stood apart and took a stand for God's purposes, even in something seemingly as small as a diet change. It wasn't small to Daniel, however, because of how he viewed his body and his purpose. And since he proved faithful and wise in the little things, he was given more favor, power, and responsibility while in the king's service.

Daniel's way of eating is an effective fast for us because it is such a shock to our systems. It's a departure from what we are used to feeding ourselves. It becomes a sacrifice and can be inconvenient for us because unlike Daniel and friends, we're not sitting in a palace having our food brought to us. We have to go out and live full lives. Committing means planning and preparation. It means thinking ahead. It means saying no when we are at work and the break room is full of goodies. But the same concept applies; it is better for us in the long run. Doing this kind of fast in the beginning of the year can be a great way to redirect our attention back to God's will and purpose for our lives. It's a great way to remember that we are still His and still sacred and set aside for His use. We are important. Our hearts have to be focused on being used by God and not being ritualistically good, though. It's what comes out that defiles a man rather than what goes in, according to Jesus. We're not looking to Daniel's point that vegetables and water are better. They are, but if you are eating well for the sake of being good or right or elitist without having God behind it, you need to check your heart condition and your motives. Be careful with that. It's easy to justify ourselves, and that's different than presenting ourselves as a living sacrifice. Lower and humble, ready for use is the goal.

Discipline is not the same as deprivation. According to Google Dictionary, deprivation is "the lack or denial of something considered to be a necessity." And we all know junk food is not a necessity. Discipline is not merely a punishment, either. Put simply: discipline is caring. It is using wisdom to not allow yourself to go down a path that will eventually lead to your destruction. It is an intentional preventative measure. But also, it is an indication of hope. If you have a vision of and a desire for a better future, you exercise discipline to make sure that when you get there it looks like what you saw in your vision. Lastly, discipline is the evidence of love.

Look at Hebrews 12:5-6 (NLT):

"And have you forgotten the encouraging words God spoke to you as his children?
He said,
'My child, don't make light of the LORD's discipline,
and don't give up when he corrects you.
For the LORD disciplines those he loves,
and he punishes each one he accepts as his child.'

As you endure this divine discipline, remember that God is treating you as His own child. Who ever heard of a child who is never disciplined by its father? If God doesn't discipline you as He does all of his children, it means that you are illegitimate and are not really His child at all. Since we respected our earthly fathers who disciplined us, shouldn't we submit even more to the discipline of the Father of our spirits and live forever?

For our earthly fathers disciplined us for a few years, doing the best they knew how. But God's discipline is always good for us, so that we might share in his holiness. **No discipline is enjoyable while it is happening—it's painful! But afterward there will be a peaceful harvest of right living for those who are trained in this way.**

So take a new grip with your tired hands and strengthen your weak knees. Mark out a straight path for your feet so that those who are weak and lame will not fall but become strong" (emphasis mine).

Read that last line again. Remember, nothing we experience or endure is for our benefit alone. It does us good to be disciplined, but it brings God glory. Through our hard-fought battles, those who aren't as strong as us can come behind us, use what we learned, and become better themselves. Isn't that the whole point of this book? Getting over your weight and into your purpose means that you're committing to prioritize God's will, the plan and future that He has for you over everything, including your diet.

Food isn't bad. But clearly, there are foods that are better for us than others. Eating the better foods help us to be sharper and healthier and keeps us in great condition to be used for God's service. When you have to make the choice between good-tasting food and food that's good for you, think about the mission and not the moment. Those snacks might be good to you right then and there, but those snacks ain't loyal. Betray your snacks. Betray them before you betray yourself, your health, your family, and your destiny.

If you find it incredibly hard to change your eating habits, remember that you don't have to do it alone. Self-control is a fruit of the Spirit. According to 1 Timothy 2:7, we've also been given the spirit of self-control (along with power and love).

Where we are weak, we can tap into God. Start by making it a habit to pray even before you choose what you will eat. I'm not talking about saying grace, because sometimes by the time we're saying grace, it's too late. We took the wrong fork in the road and want God to cover it. How many times have you prayed "let it be nourishing for my body" over some food that it would literally take a miracle to find a vitamin, mineral, or nutrient in? Yes, give thanks, always. But what I am recommending is that we invite God into every step of this meal planning process. Invite Him in because He will show you grace and mercy and give you wisdom and strength.

What's It Going to Be?

Turn on any streaming service and you'll find hundreds of documentaries on our food. They educate us on the ways it's made, the ways it is grown, the history of it, and the politics behind it. There are many perspectives on what's best or worst for our bodies, our health, and our weight. There are many agendas and industries that stand to benefit (or lose) from a large-scale shift in perspective. And yet that are also many well-meaning, well-studied, passionate people who only seek to inform us of what they've discovered simply because they are trying to help. There many differing and conflicting views, and yet everyone holds the view that she or he is right. So who do we believe? How do we know what's right?

I can't answer that question. Personally, before writing this book, I would swing from one diet or program to the next. There are many different ways of eating for weight loss and general health. What I've learned is to pick one or two that will be sustainable for you and that work best for your body. I have learned to stop feeling bullied or pressured into anything else. And I definitely don't feel judged by anyone's differing perspective anymore. People's opinions often change. For instance, we have shopped at the grocery store Aldi since my childhood. So without issue, we continued to shop there after Ray and I were married. Friends and family would often come over to our home, open our fridge, notice the lack of name brands, and immediately start to pity or judge us. Meanwhile, our grocery bills were beautiful, and we saved money to apply to things like vacation or big ticket purchases. Culture said to buy name-brand food then, but now shopping at Aldi is the move. Currently, many of the popular bloggers and influencers are shopping there, and other people are being exposed and influenced to follow suit. It doesn't affect me one way or the other because I knew my reason for shopping there, and it worked for my family. The same goes for the way that you eat. You want to make a lifestyle change, not go on a diet. You need balance. You need fuel for the road ahead. Whatever way of eating gets you in the best condition to fulfill your purpose is the one you should go with without guilt, shame, or hesitation. Don't be quick to jump on the next and newest fad, especially if what you are doing is yielding the results you desire. You may have to do some research on your own, but here are just some of the different methods of eating that I've come across that you should inquire with God about trying:

- Vegan
- Vegetarian
- Pescatarian

- Fruitarian
- Eating for your blood type
- Intermittent fasting
- Ketogenic
- Low-carb
- Gluten-free
- Low-sugar
- Paleo
- Mediterranean
- Ayurvedic
- Calorie-counting

Ask God how your diet is supposed to look for your work and your purpose.

Perhaps the best example I can find is, of course, Biblical. It's in the stories of cousins Jesus Christ and John the Baptist. Jesus said himself, "For John didn't spend his time eating and drinking, and you say, 'He's possessed by a demon.' The Son of Man, on the other hand, feasts and drinks, and you say, 'He's a glutton and a drunkard, and a friend of tax collectors and other sinners!' But wisdom is shown to be right by its results'" Matthew 11:19 (NLT).

Both Jesus and John had a similar message of repentance because the Kingdom of Heaven was/is near. They both had followers and large crowds travel from far and wide to see them on a daily basis. They both were intent on living out and fulfilling their purposes. But their methods and their diets looked different from one another. John ate locusts and honey out in the wilderness, while Jesus dined on what others were eating and even kept some questionable company (by the standards of the religious leaders of the time). Some even questioned *why* Jesus and His disciples ate *when* they did (accusing them of breaking Jewish laws and traditions). People held opinions and made assumptions, but regardless, both John and Jesus made an impact and fulfilled the purpose for which they were sent. So, with that in mind, spend less time trying to get it right or approved by others. Don't worry about other people and their opinions. If God gives you the vision and the instructions to accompany that vision, it's not for people to understand what you're doing or why. It's important that you be obedient. You'll bear the fruit of that obedience in due time.

Ultimately, in my opinion, when it comes to eating for weight loss, it all boils down to calories in, calories out. Simply put: you have to eat fewer calories than you burn off to lose weight. The overall goal is to feel great and be at your peak performance. If your diet is making you too tired, too cranky, and too obsessed to have peace for extended periods of time, then you have to do something different. One of the best methods for me has been to simply crowd out my unwise food choices with better ones. I've never been the person to whip out a garbage bag and clear the food out of my entire kitchen. First of all, I'm way too frugal for that. Instead, I started with breakfast and used the crowd out method. In the place of cheesy eggs with a bagel and cream cheese, I added vegetables to my eggs and had a slice of toast. I thoroughly enjoy breads, cakes, and brownies. If I tried to quit them cold turkey, I would probably not last past 1:00 p.m. So by substituting with a healthier choice or version of that food, I don't feel as deprived, but I do feel better about the healthier choice I made. That inspires me to continue during the next meal. You can try making subtle, sustainable changes like this, too. After a while, you'll realize you have very little space or need for unhealthy choices.

Bottom line: don't fall in love with your method. The main goal of this journey is to dethrone weight loss and to put God back in His rightful position. So if you find something that works for you, don't in turn start to worship the method you used. I know you've seen it: someone loses some weight by going vegan, for example, and now they judge every piece of meat that passes their friends' lips. They become vegan elitists, vegan evangelists, telling everyone every chance they get about how good vegan is and how good it's been to them. And they may be truly sincere in wanting to help others change their lives, too. They could just be happy that they have finally found something that works. I get that. The problem occurs when we're so devoted to the method that we get distracted from doing the work we are supposed to be doing for God. It's just a tool.

Remember it's not always about what you eat; sometimes it's about why you're eating. Beyond cravings, slow down and ask yourself *why* you are choosing to eat what you are eating.

Remember, you have authority. Eat with purpose. Be faithful in small things. Plan, prepare, pray, and push yourself to stay on the path. What is your why? Write it down and stick it on your refrigerator or tape it to the inside of your cabinets. Having reminders around you can encourage you to stay faithful. Pay attention to how you feel, too (physically and emotionally). Feelings can often drive our food choices, so identify other ways to destress and decompress. Track and prepare for your PMS. Many pans of brownies have fallen victim to my hormones in the past, but there are better ways to quench chocolate cravings. (I've discovered a bomb chocolate quinoa granola mix that hits the spot and gives me some protein as a bonus.)

Food is a mood-altering substance. For that reason, I often have to remind myself to use food for nutrition and not comfort. I have always disagreed that I have been an emotional eater in the past because I didn't turn to certain unhealthy foods when I was experiencing extreme moods like sadness or depression. I don't eat my emotions, but I get emotional when I eat. Listen, brownies make me happy, even if I'm not sad to begin with. I bite them and experience joy.

You have to be conscious and evaluate the what, when, why, where, and how of your food choices.

Some days I really, really, really crave fast food. I know it's terrible for me. I know it's cheap trash devoid of nutrients and filled with preservatives. I know I'm better than that, and I know I am worth more.

But, um, have you ever tasted it? Fast food is delicious.

Secret Donuts

In addition to secret donuts, for years, I've been having secret combos, too. I would do fast food runs in the morning or during the workday because it's more convenient, and I can just jump right into work or not have to stop my flow. One day, I took a look at my bank account. I added up a month's worth of my fast food. After doing all of the math, I found that although the food was cheap as individual line items, together it was a big expense. When I added the monthly costs, they equated to a plane ticket, home decor items I'd been eyeing, or money I could simply be saving for a rainy day.

So, I started to tell myself the narrative that I cannot afford fast food. Although I really can afford fast food, I cannot afford to not reach my goals financially, physically, and internally. When looking at it from that perspective, it became way too expensive on so many different levels to continue to eat fast food. So when the urge comes to stop and just grab a whatever, I will recite this line aloud to myself: "I'm not going to squander my family's wealth $10 at a time. There are so many different goals for which we can use this money." I mean, imagine struggling to pay for my brilliant son's college tuition because I just had to have that four-for-four in 2018. Those two lines jolt me back into reality and help me see the big picture. It helps me to see what's important. It encourages me to act like what I ask for. If I asked for help from God or from others in the areas of food choices and finances, then I need to respect their time, wisdom, and resources.

While we're on the subject: stop asking for help you don't really want. Don't go to a nutritionist, don't join an accountability group, don't go to a physical trainer, and don't get a gym membership if you're not in agreement with the person or organization that you're hiring to help you get this area of your life together. Don't make investments and commitments simply because they seem like the right things to do at the time. If you have not made a heart commitment to it, then don't make any kind of commitment to it except to investigate why you can't or won't fully commit your heart. Get to the root issue. If you make a move before you do, you may be less likely to see changes that last. You will end up discouraged and with the false narrative that you can't do it. You can! The Bible says, "Can two people walk together without agreeing on the direction?" (Amos 3:3 NIV). You can't blame someone else for not doing the part that you're supposed to do. The person from whom you're seeking help and/or advice is not in charge of you. You're in charge. You are the main decision-maker, so you can't blame that person when you don't make the decision to change and changes don't happen. If you're not getting results, it could very well be because of how you think rather than what you're doing. Other people can believe in you, but they can't believe *for* you. As a person who gives a lot of advice, there are few things more annoying than sharing some wisdom, having a person say, "Okay! Yeah, you're right!" but then not apply a thing that you said (or take any other action for that matter). After a while, they find themselves in the same situation and calling me again for the same advice I already gave them. It's a waste of time, it's a waste of energy, and it almost feels like disrespect. If you are not ready to change, take the steps to get your mindset right. This book is a great start. I recommend adding to it regular quiet time, prayer, reading your Bible, and going to therapy.

Once you're clear on how loved you are just as you are, I think that that's the safest time to seek to lose weight. Agreeing that your value isn't determined by how you look and that no one can accept or reject you on that basis will empower you with peace and positivity. You'll have a strong foundation of unconditional love for yourself and motivation to see your efforts through. You'll be able to love yourself *while* you are losing weight, not *because* you are losing weight.

You are and have always been more than what you weigh.

We're Almost There

AFTERWORD

My Before and After

We started this book talking about donuts, and I'm going to end there, too. Do I still have donuts? Yes. Do I eat them as often? No. Do I still eat them in secret? Sometimes. Old habits die hard, so it has been a process. I will keep working on it.

Over the course of this year and while writing this book, I've worked out more, eaten better, and loved and enjoyed myself and my life more than any other year prior. I've bought myself more clothes within a couple of months than I had within an entire year's span in the past. I've been exploring style and buying the right (read: bigger) size clothes for the better fit. I used to look at plus-sized fashion models and influencers and think that that's nice for them that they are willing and able to be fly while fat, but I wasn't. Now I know that style transcends size, and I don't have to wait. Big or small, I'm allowed to slay. I've enjoyed doing my makeup and getting my hair done (and even took steps to successfully heal my alopecia—a whole different story). Those are just the external changes.

I literally feel the liberation that comes with real, authentic, Christ-centered self-love. I feel more like myself than I have felt in a very long time. I go out, I show up, I don't linger in the shadows. My confidence has skyrocketed. All of this because I said, "Yes."

Wow, God.

You want to know what's crazy? I've experienced all of the growth, attitude changes, actions, hope, and faith through that "Yes," but this year, I haven't lost a single pound. In fact, I *gained* weight. In fact, as I am writing this, I weigh about six pounds less than I weighed at my heaviest (while nine months pregnant with my first kid). All of the changes I made this year scientifically should have led to weight loss. I did a 30-day workout challenge, exercising consistently for 30 days, and gained 10 pounds. I did a Daniel Fast for 16 days, and the scale didn't move. I believe it's because of the commitment I made to not focus on losing weight this year. God blocked my distractions. He even blocked the distraction of success so that I could hear Him clearly, so that I could trust in Him solely, so that I could experience Him fully, and so that I could write this book genuinely.

Over this process, I've been tempted to delay writing this book because I felt like I needed to write from a space of expertise. I felt that I needed to go out and lose weight first so that I could come back, write this book, and say to all of you, "Follow me!" while leading the way. Instead, through God's grace and infinite wisdom, I was given this space to renew my mind, to heal, to trust, to share, and to connect. He gave me the understanding to know that the best possible declaration for me will always be "Let's follow Him!" while He leads the way. Matthew 6:33 was demonstrated so thoroughly for me in this season. I've sought after God, His purpose, His will, and His presence and received a peace I've never experienced.

Secret Donuts

I believed I needed a before-and-after story of transformation, and that's what I received. It's wasn't what I planned or expected, but this truly exceeded my expectation.

There's no doubt in my mind that soon you'll see me and I will be smaller. I have no desire to strive to lose weight, but the mental lightness I feel sparks the motivation I've lacked in the past to be more intentional about taking care of myself. When you love and you're kind to yourself, you instinctually treat yourself better. Beyond that, I'm excited about my future and about what God will do through me. My willingness to be obedient to my purpose and His timing are even stronger now, at this weight, than I imagined it would be had I gotten those 80 (now 90) pounds off.

It is my sincere hope that along our journey together, you've come to understand even more about our all-knowing, all-seeing, trustworthy, loving, patient God. I hope that you have been inspired to dig deeper into the Word and spend time in prayer to get to know Him even better. I pray that you can trust Him enough to remove your obsession with weight loss from the throne of your life and put Him on it. It's my prayer that you fully understand how much you mean to God and how much He absolutely loves you at this very moment (just as you are). I pray that through this book, you've discovered and internalized your identity through Christ. I also pray that you have been freed from the bondage of obsessing over your weight and from the fear of rejection so that you can get to the purpose to which God has called you. Most of all, I pray that my transparency, my transformation, and my testimony have inspired you to give Him your "Yes." No matter how weird the assignment or command, no matter how you feel, no matter what you've learned and no matter what any else says, I pray that you will simply trust Him. He has a specific plan for you. You think you know how it will pan out. He *actually knows* how it will pan out. Trust Him.

The journey isn't over, but this is where we part ways. Don't stop here, friend. Keep going forward and I will, too.
No more secrets. No more shame.
Just love.

About the Author

Alicia Watson is a Maryland-based cinematographer and photographer. She has degrees in Communication & Media Studies and Sociology from University of Michigan. A passionate storyteller, she started as an actor and playwright and evolved into owning and operating Ali Watson Media, a boutique digital media company focused on helping small business and entrepreneurs brand visually and authentically.

Through being a writer, filmmaker, playwright, speaker, and now author, Alicia draws on her gifts of empathy and optimism to connect visionary, purpose-seeking believers to the truth we have in Christ. Alicia is married to her husband, Raymond Jr., and has two children—Raymond III and Reagan. She spends her downtime traveling, decorating her home, creating with her husband, and managing her children's social and activity calendars.

To learn more, visit www.aliciawatson.com

CREATING DISTINCTIVE BOOKS
WITH INTENTIONAL RESULTS

We're a collaborative group of creative masterminds with a mission to produce high-quality books to position you for monumental success in the marketplace.

Our professional team of writers, editors, designers, and marketing strategists work closely together to ensure that every detail of your book is a clear representation of the message in your writing.

Want to know more?
Write to us at info@publishyourgift.com
or call (888) 949-6228

Discover great books, exclusive offers, and more at
www.PublishYourGift.com

Connect with us on social media

@publishyourgift

www.ingramcontent.com/pod-product-compliance
Lightning Source LLC
Chambersburg PA
CBHW052133110526
44591CB00012B/1706